"The compassion and empathy of Jes[...] it will undoubtedly comfort you. Fo[...] [...]ave experienced deep heartache, and for any who have walked with friends through unimaginable grief, the gems in this book are more precious than gold. Here is wisdom for our sorrows and solace for our pains. Very few people get through this life unscathed by suffering, and *Just Be Honest* helps us grasp that reality that Jesus is 'hospitable to heartache' and that 'hurting people need to be heard.' Absorbing and applying these truths can save your faith and help you brave the brokenness of life with those you love. Whether you are amid sorrow currently, preparing for sorrow eventually, or walking with others through their sorrows sympathetically, this book will prove to be a masterful guide!"

CRAIG ALLEN COOPER, *USA Today* Best-Selling Author, *Glad You're Here: Two Unlikely Friends Breaking Bread and Fences* (with Walker Hayes); Author, *Overflowing Mercies: 100 Meditations on the Tender Heart of God*

"With pastoral tenderness and wisdom, Clint Watkins shares how the practice of honest lament was the grace he needed to draw near to God in a time of acute pain and heartache. Watkins compels us to make space in our personal lives and faith communities for worship practices that engage the whole spectrum of human longing and need. In an age when we're rewarded for putting our best selves forward, *Just Be Honest* is not a blueprint for a better way but an invitation to enter one."

ADRIEL BOOKER, Author, *Grace Like Scarlett* and *Tethered to Hope*

"Why do I presume that faith means pretending that the Christian life is always cheery and fulfilling? Through his careful unfolding of the biblical witness on lament and complaint, Watkins extended to me the Lord's permission both to grieve and grieve like a Christian. I suspect he'll do the same for you."

PETER KROL, President, DiscipleMakers campus ministry

"Clint helps readers discover a legacy of lament that allows us to hope through heartache and trust through tears. Clint has known loss that cannot be assuaged by Christian platitudes, yet he writes beautifully of the consolation he found when he broke his silence with Jesus, the one 'acquainted with grief.'"

PETER GREER, CEO, HOPE International; Co-author, *Mission Drift: The Unspoken Crisis Facing Leaders, Charities, and Churches*

"When we cannot reconcile our experience of tragedy with our faith in the God who could have prevented it, what happens next? Clint Watkins bravely wades into the tension between doubt and faith, helping show a faithful way through questions and pain for those of us who feel too afraid, too weak, or too bitter to even dip our toe in. Through artfully constructed sentences and beautifully presented personal experience, *Just Be Honest* provides a much needed alternative to 'faking it till you make it' or abandoning faith because belief feels too hard. What an incredible gift to the weary minds and vulnerable hearts of sufferers."

ABBEY WEDGEWORTH, Author, *Held* and the Training Young Hearts children's book series

"Our God can handle periods on the ends of our sentences of pain. 'I'm devastated.' 'We're reeling.' 'Honestly, I'm really struggling.' He feels no anxiety to immediately relieve the tension. He is not too fragile for our faith to be fragile. Yet some of us feel the pressure to leave no more than commas, if we leave room for any pause at all. Meanwhile the spirit of our age evokes complaining, wallowing, and unbelief. How might we learn to lament faithfully, as Christians? Clint Watkins has suffered deeply, thought deeply, and knows the deep, deep love of Jesus. Let him share his scarred and recovering soul— and his scarred and majestic consoling King. Jesus does not commend doubt but calls and welcomes us to bring it to him. He gives not only joy in place of pain, but joy deeper than pain in the midst of it. He is a king who can handle your periods, your pauses, and your process."

DAVID MATHIS, Senior Teacher and Executive Editor, desiringGod.org; Pastor, Cities Church; Author, *Rich Wounds: The Countless Treasures of the Life, Death, and Triumph of Jesus*

"*Just Be Hones*t is a rare treasure: a book on suffering I would actually dare to give someone in the midst of their pain. Heart-wrenchingly honest about how faith is no stranger to deep pain and how Scripture refuses to oversimplify the struggle with anguish in our souls, this book will connect to the Lord hearts shattered by countless griefs by teaching the piercing, soul-sustaining path of lament."

J. ALASDAIR GROVES, Executive Director, CCEF (Christian Counseling and Educational Foundation); Co-author, *Untangling Emotions*

JUST
BE
HONEST

*How to Worship
through Tears
and Pray
without
Pretending*

CLINT WATKINS

For our little warrior,
Eli David Watkins.
(Psalm 127:3)

Just Be Honest
© DiscipleMakers 2024

Published by:
The Good Book Company

thegoodbook.com | thegoodbook.co.uk
thegoodbook.com.au | thegoodbook.co.nz | thegoodbook.co.in

ISBN: 9781784988951 | JOB-007582 | Printed in India

Cover design by Drew McCall

CONTENTS

FOREWORD

by Vaneetha Risner

Suffering has a way of reframing everything we once held dear. The biblical truths we have long believed can suddenly feel hollow as we find ourselves grappling with a dilemma: how can we find comfort in the very God who could heal our deepest wounds with a word, yet seemingly chooses not to? We start wondering if God even cares about our pain—but that wondering seems too scandalous to voice.

In these pages, Clint Watkins illuminates a path less traveled—a path of honest wrestling with God through lament. He vulnerably invites us into his inner life, to see the raw reality of pain and loss and what it looks like to engage with God without denying our intense hurts. When we do, we discover that the Israelites, God's Old Testament people, were accustomed to wrestling with

God as a regular part of praise and worship. In fact, the very name Israel means "one who struggles with God." They found solace in a God who didn't simply endure their mournful cries but rather welcomed their lament, regarding it as part of worship.

I wish I had had this book when I first encountered loss. I buried my infant son when he was two months old due to a doctor's careless mistake, and in the weeks and months that followed I had no categories for how to process such a profound loss. While I'd faithfully spoken of God's goodness at Paul's funeral, weeks later I saw no shred of that goodness in my life.

I was lost. Wondering what to hold onto. Not sure who to trust with the growing sense of feeling betrayed, abandoned, and forgotten by God. I wondered why God hadn't answered my prayers: those desperate pleas I poured out while kneeling till my body ached, begging him to spare my son.

There were few people I could talk to about how I was feeling. I had been teaching Bible study at our church and assumed people were watching me closely, judging me by the orthodoxy of my response. I thought strong faith meant never questioning God, that it had to look like boldly praising him as my world was ripped apart.

So I said the right thing, thinking that it was my job to defend God. I assumed that letting people know I was struggling would damage their faith. It was a twisted way of thinking, but I felt responsible for what other people thought about God. And that sense of responsibility led me to pretend I was ok when I was dying inside. It pushed me away from facing my own emotions. It pushed me away from community. Most importantly, it pushed me away from God.

I discovered the grace of lament when I was well into my journey of grief, and it became a lifeline for me as I weathered subsequent losses. A diagnosis of post-polio syndrome which may eventually leave me a quadriplegic. Betrayal and an unwanted divorce after 20 years of marriage. Raising two angry adolescents as a single parent. I remember screaming into my pillow many nights—and also in front of my pastor—"Why does God hate me?"

It was through those honest exchanges that I discovered that not only does God not hate me but he loves me extravagantly. But that discovery was a process, one that required I be "all in" with God—wrestling with him, engaging my fears and questions, confessing my doubts and anger. I needed to know that even in my worst moments, in my bursts of uncontrolled emotion and angry tears, I was safe. That I could cry out to God with my greatest hurts, knowing he was holding me, inviting me into a richer life with him.

So I wish I had had this book for those times. *Just Be Honest* is a masterful testimony to that mysterious process in which we offer God our questions and doubts and inexplicably emerge with a stronger faith than we could have imagined. With insight and compassion, Clint confronts our tendency to "wrap up stories of suffering with lessons and silver linings." Instead, he invites us to sit with our sorrow and to bring our pain before the Lord without pretense. He presents a compelling case, rooted in Scripture, that the strongest faith may involve honest struggle, and that the deepest trust may be forged in the fire of our doubts.

As you embark on this journey through the exquisite and soul-stirring pages that follow, may you find the courage to embrace your own wrestling with God. May you discover that your weeping is not weak and that your wrestling is not irreverent. May you find comfort in knowing that Jesus, who himself offered his own prayers with loud tears, will be your tender companion through every trial. And may you experience the transformative power of lament, allowing it to deepen your worship and strengthen your walk with the Lord.

Vaneetha Risner
Author, *The Scars That Have Shaped Me* and *Desperate for Hope*
July 2023

HURTING WITH GOD

Flip through my Bible and, at first, you won't notice anything unusual. Its weathered pages bear the typical signs of a well-worn book. But find your way to the book of Lamentations—to the empty space after its final verse—and you will see a striking addition: the footprints of our firstborn son. Black ink, provided by the hospital after he was born, captured an impression of his particular beauty. Distinct lines. Delicate ridges. Marks made permanent by his soles and toes. These tiny footprints always stir my fatherly pride. But they also provoke unspeakable pain. Due to a fatal condition, our son did not survive—his birth and his death occurred in the same room. My Bible is one of the only surfaces ever touched by the feet of our son, Eli.

We found out Eli's diagnosis months before he was born. A routine anatomy scan turned my wife's first pregnancy from wonder to terror—a medical condition which we had never heard of introduced an agony we had never known. The doctors told us that our son would continue growing in the womb but would not live after delivery. Jillian would endure the discomfort of pregnancy and the excruciating pain of labor. But we would not come home with our son.

Preparing for Eli's birth was unbearable. Before we had even met our baby, we had to prepare our goodbye. We exchanged nursery plans for funeral arrangements. Instead of a crib, we chose a casket. I longed for the chance to hold my child but dreaded the horror of letting him go. Agony strangled my soul as I could do nothing to save my son or protect my wife from devastation. I was a shell of a husband, a shadow of a father. Despite the despair, we fought to cherish every moment and memory we could steal back with our son during the pregnancy. But sorrow eclipsed each glimpse of joy as every day crept toward our loss.

I've never had such intense conflict with the Lord as in that season. I still believed he was sovereign and good. But his good promises felt hollow and his sovereign plan seemed harsh. Gospel truths that I had championed for years as a missionary now rang trite and ineffective. I clung to the promise that only the Lord could offer hope for my withering heart. Yet how could I find refuge in the one who had the power to heal my son but chose not to? It was not well with my soul.

You may have picked up this book because you're feeling something similar. Your circumstances are likely different, but the sting of your spiritual pain is the same: "Where is God? Why is he allowing this? Lord, why don't you do something?" And then guilt whispers to your soul: "Am I allowed to say these things? Shouldn't I trust God without hesitation? Am I just a faithless Christian?" Suffering can reduce your prayers to questions. And shame tries to convince you that your questions are unwelcome.

Christian culture can reinforce the pressure we feel to appear composed through our suffering. Conflict with the Lord doesn't always seem to have a place in church. Instead, spiritual positivity dominates the landscape. We're quick to point to a God who is in control, but slow to wrestle with the tension that this truth entails. People feel obligated to wrap up their stories of suffering with lessons and silver linings. Prayers often ring out with declarations of trust and polite petitions. And the majority of our songs resound with victorious joy. Belief, then, becomes synonymous with optimism—relegating sorrow to the fringes of faith.

I felt this acutely in church following Eli's diagnosis. While song after song of joy surrounded us, the best I could do was suppress my weeping. This tearful silence became my common posture during worship. I ached for lyrics and prayers that would give voice to our pain and wrestling with God, but what I longed for didn't seem to exist. Instead, triumphant prayers defeated me. Uplifting choruses brought me further down. Apparently, I had not been given the kind of faith that produces happy praise in the midst of pain. And I was neither able nor willing to pretend otherwise.

But what if I told you that there's another way to relate to God in suffering? You don't need to choose between silence or optimism. You can wrestle honestly with God through lament.

Lament was how sufferers in the Bible struggled in the tension between their pain and God's promises. From Genesis to Revelation, burdened believers groaned boldly before the Lord: heartfelt cries about hardship, probing questions about God's involvement, and desperate pleas for his intervention. Scripture shows us that faith doesn't have to be tied up neatly—it is often knotted with tension. The believers of old did, indeed, praise the Lord. However, their praise was filled with God-wrestling. And engaging God with their hurts was what paved the way for lasting hope.

The Lord didn't merely tolerate these cries; he authorized lament as an act of worship. And he still does. God welcomes his people to worship through tears and pray without pretending. Aches, questions, and tears are a heritage of faith handed down to us through the generations. We belong to a legacy of lament.

Today, however, lament has become a forgotten refrain. A language that God's people were fluent in for millennia has now become foreign for many. My aim in this book is to help you recover God's gift of honest wrestling. The Lord does not expect you to simply polish your pain with his promises or raise a hallelujah over your hurts. Nor does he require you to leave your sorrow at home on Sundays. You can seize hope by voicing your heartache to the Lord.

We're going to explore how God's invitation to be honest about suffering (chapter 1) is demonstrated and authorized by Jesus (chapter 2). Learning to lament (chapter 3) can keep us from grumbling (chapter 4) and help us rejoice in suffering (chapter 5). When we lament as communities in worship (chapter 6) and rely on others in our pain (chapter 7), we can fulfill our call to weep with those who weep (chapter 8).

So if you picked up this book because you are hurting, I hope you find that Scripture gives voice to your sorrow. God invites you to come to him with all your questions and uncertainties. Or you may be reading because you know someone who is currently suffering, and you want to be able to respond well to them. I trust this book will help you walk with them in their darkness. Whatever season you're in, I pray that you will discover God's gift of lament, and feel better equipped to help others do the same.

My prayer for you as you read is rooted in our son's name. Eli means, "my God," a phrase found in many prayers throughout Scripture. Sometimes it's a confident declaration, other times it's a cry of despair. It's how Jesus called out from the cross as he died. "My God, my God, why have you forsaken me?" (Matthew 27:46). Every time we utter a lament like this, it is a prayer of both dependence and desperation. Whenever my wife and I say the words "Eli," the gospel whispers alongside his name—the story of a consoling King who knows our pain and hears our cries. I pray that you discover the hope to be found by honestly crying out, "My God."

I printed Eli's ink-covered feet in the book of Lamentations because it's one of many places in the Bible where personal pain collides with God's promises. I hope that you, too, will find that God's word speaks for your wounds.

BEING

HONEST

WITH

GOD

PART 1

CHAPTER 1

STRONG FAITH
STRUGGLES

Weeping and writhing on the floor—this is how I broke two months of silence with God.

This moment was preceded by weeks of escalating tension. In the days after learning Eli's diagnosis, my ability to face God faded. Though I knew that Jesus was with us and for us, that we would endure by the help of his Spirit and with the support of our community, and that the Lord would somehow work this terrible loss for good in eternity—our son was going to die. And that agony extinguished my capacity for prayer.

It hurt too much to hold God's gaze. I couldn't turn his way. I needed space. But I also knew I needed him. So after weeks of avoidance, I entered the ring with God. A retreat to a cabin in the woods ensured that no one else would be disturbed by the commotion.

There, the tension erupted. I bombarded heaven with my heartache.

You can't miss this altercation when flipping through my journal. Pages of neatly processed pain are interrupted by a sheet of smeared ramblings. Smudged prayers, half-finished phrases, pieces of songs, fragmented Bible verses—all scratched in the middle of a notebook to keep their memory close. I even scribbled a timeline of those grueling hours and noted how my body had disrupted the dust on the floor.

Every detail was important. I did not want to forget this encounter.

Some might want to keep the spotlight away from this scene... A 28-year-old man rendered useless by sorrow. A missionary who avoided the Lord for months. A prayer that was more confrontation than conversation. A person of faith with no faith left—or so it seemed.

Except that when you page through the Bible, you'll be frequently confronted by experiences like mine. Prayers of pain punctuate the plotline. Sorrowful saints cry out from the storm. Even heroes of faith fall apart.

These episodes surprise us because we tend to equate strong faith with confidence and composure. Though we ache and sigh and worry and fear, we hide our hurts behind polite spirituality and courageous belief. But dry eyes are not a tell-tale sign of strong faith. Some of the most steadfast believers look at the world through tears and walk with a limp.

You might be tempted to erase the scenes in your story where you've wept and wrestled with God. But the Lord treasures dented and messy faith. We'll see in this chapter that he doesn't filter out struggle—so neither should we.

STRONG FAITH WEEPS

We typically have a difficult time with difficult emotions. Put simply, it doesn't feel good to feel bad. Sadness, anger, and anxiety are feelings we try to overcome quickly or avoid altogether. And in many parts of Christian culture there's an imbalance towards positivity, progress, and praise. As a result, unpleasant emotions make us feel uncomfortable *and* unfaithful; sorrow seems incompatible with trust in God.

Scripture, however, takes you across a different landscape. There, men and women grapple with things like depression, despair, and doubt. But they don't conceal their struggles or rush towards a happy ending. They sit with their sorrow, talk openly about their difficulties, and bring their pain before the Lord. The way they speak so freely about their heartache defies the notion that strong believers always stay poised under pressure. But their sorrow is by no means a lack of faith. Rather, it's their robust belief in God that drives them to engage with him and express their deepest hurts.

Israel's exodus story calls for our attention. You might remember how, after their rescue, they descended into sinful grumbling in the wilderness. But it's easy to forget how their story began—faithful groaning. The opening chapters of Exodus introduce a tragic situation. Israel is enslaved to a ruthless king who plots to kill their newborn sons. But God's people do not settle for platitudes like "everything happens for a reason" or that "God won't give you more than you can handle." No, they "groaned because of their slavery and cried out for help. Their cry for rescue from slavery came up to God. And God heard their groaning, and God remembered his covenant" (Exodus 2:23-24). The Lord was not moved to act because of stoic faith, but loud cries. Lamentation prompted liberation.

You can hear whispers of Exodus if you turn to Matthew's Christmas story. We often decorate the holiday season with cheer and wonder. But not everyone was "joyful and triumphant" in the wake of Jesus' birth. When news of a newborn Messiah reached the palace, another heartless king turned to violence. In an attempt to kill Jesus, King Herod took the lives of innocent children. Matthew tells us the resulting chorus was one of "weeping and loud lamentation" (Matthew 2:18). This night was not silent, calm, or bright. One of the first Christmas carols was a hymn of heartache composed by grieving parents.

But it's not only communal cries that we hear in the story of God's people. Zoom in on individuals and you will see the same willingness to weep.

As Hannah lamented her inability to conceive, she "was deeply distressed and prayed to the Lord and wept bitterly" (1 Samuel 1:10). When David grieved the deaths of Israel's king and prince, he led God's people in mourning by writing a lament that was taught across the nation and remembered forever (2 Samuel 1:11-27). As Asaph's sorrow kept him from sleeping, he cried, "My soul refuses to be comforted" (Psalm 77:2). When Mary met Jesus after her brother's death, she fell at his feet and wept (John 11:32-33). And the apostle Paul spoke of "great sorrow and unceasing anguish in [his] heart" (Romans 9:2) on behalf of others.

We have only skimmed the surface of these stories, but each glimpse is part of a greater picture: faith does not erase sorrow. Whether it's the loss of a dream or the death of a loved one, the pain of isolation or the weight of despair, the Bible repeatedly shows that faithful men and women cry out honestly to the Lord. The authors of *Untangling Emotions* put it this way:

> *Unlike our assumption that the most faithful people will be the most carefree and emotionally upbeat, Scripture is full of aching, grieving saints who tear their clothes and sit in the ashes when their world gets upended. The basic logic in the Bible is this: if you care about others and the kingdom and mission of God in this world, you will be **and you should be** full of sorrow when you or those you love are injured, suffer loss, or die.*[1]

Do you ever feel burdened by the pain in and around you? Does your soul ever ache as you long for God to restore what is broken? You do not need to hide your hurts or silence your sadness. Scripture urges you to engage your difficult emotions and express your inward groanings.

Put simply, "The Bible schools us to pray with blistering honesty."[2] Instead of avoiding heartache, God's word urges you—*lean in*. Strong faith weeps.

STRONG FAITH WRESTLES

"God is in control... It's not up to us to question God."

This well-intentioned platitude pierced my heart. It was meant to assuage the anguish of my son's death—but it provided no relief.

Why? Because it assumed that knowledge of the Lord's sovereign goodness should always result in immediate, subdued trust. Suffering is inevitable and God will work all things together for good, so why would we question his presence, power, or plan?

Such reasoning sounds noble, which is what makes platitudes so deceptive—they're veiled in spirituality. And while the Lord sometimes gives people surprising peace in the storm, Scripture also shows that authentic faith can involve frequent struggle. Over and over again, sufferers bring God not only their tears but also their questions and complaints. To our surprise, the Lord does not turn them away. He graciously invites their wrestling.

Consider Abraham, who we meet in Genesis 12. God said "Go," and Abraham went (Genesis 12:1, 4). He "obeyed when he was called ... not knowing where he was going" (Hebrews 11:8). His instant obedience rings with the dedication we wish to imitate. Abraham believed God's outrageous promise: that he and his wife, though old and childless, would bear offspring that would become a great nation to bless the entire world (Genesis 12:2-3).

At first, we're not told much about Abraham's thinking. The first three chapters of his story pass by without describing any dialogue between him and the Lord. God simply gives orders and makes promises; Abraham trusts and obeys. But when Abraham finally speaks to God, the conversation is not what you might expect from such a devout follower.

Abraham questions God. Years have gone by and God still hasn't delivered: "O LORD God, what will you give me, for I continue childless, and the heir of my house is Eliezer of Damascus?" (Genesis 15:2). Abraham takes it upon himself to inform God of his unfulfilled promises. Time is running out. He still has no child, so his inheritance will be given to someone else. He reiterates his complaint and God's responsibility: "Behold, you have given me no offspring, and a member of my household will be my heir" (v 3). Abraham seems to weaken under the pressure of waiting.

But the New Testament says that, on the contrary, this moment reveals Abraham's unwavering faith. Romans 4 summarizes this scene by saying that "no unbelief made him waver concerning the promise of God, but he grew strong in his faith as he gave glory to God" (Romans 4:20). According to Scripture, wrestling and wavering are not one and the same—strong faith involves honest struggle.

You see a similar interaction with Moses as he leads Israel in the wilderness. In Numbers 11 the people are grumbling, God is angry, and Moses reaches the end of himself. He complains to the Lord: "Why have you dealt ill with your servant? And why have I not found favor in your sight, that you lay the burden of this people on me? ... I am not able to carry all this people alone; the burden is too heavy for me" (Number 11:11, 14). His brash prayer is that of an exhausted leader grappling with God's goodness. But the Lord does not respond with the same anger he had directed towards the disbelieving Israelites just moments before. Rather, he provides Moses with the help he needs to relieve his burden. Why does God condemn Israel's complaint but accept Moses'? We'll discuss that in Chapter 4. But for now, know this: the Lord welcomes passionate struggle.

David followed in the footsteps of Abraham and Moses, having several wrestling matches with God. Persecution, sickness, isolation, and grief fueled his questions and complaints. Listen to these snapshots of his conflicts, recorded in the book of Psalms:

How long, O LORD? Will you forget me forever? (Psalm 13:1)

Why are you so far from saving me, from the words of my groaning? (Psalm 22:1)

Look away from me, that I may smile again, before I depart and am no more! (Psalm 39:13)

Attend to me, and answer me; I am restless in my complaint and I moan. (Psalm 55:2)

Hear my voice, O God, in my complaint. (Psalm 64:1)

My eyes grow dim with waiting for my God. (Psalm 69:3)

I pour out my complaint before him; I tell my trouble before him. (Psalm 142:2)

Look to the right and see: there is none who takes notice of me; no refuge remains to me; no one cares for my soul. (Psalm 142:4)

We can rush past these lines without considering the full weight behind them. Go back and read them again. They are not polite prayers—they're emotionally charged and acutely honest. David questions God's memory, nearness, and timing. The relational tension is palpable. At one point he's exhausted from waiting on the Lord, at another he asks God for some breathing room. It's surprising to think that the Lord would tolerate such directness. It's all the more astonishing to realize that these are psalms: communal prayers passed down through the generations for all God's people to use. God established honest wrestling as a template for genuine worship.

You might be tempted to think that these are just examples of Old Testament faith—an unpolished way of relating to God before Jesus came and turned everything happy. But New Testament saints continued the legacy of God-wrestling.

Take John the Baptist, for example. His bold preaching drew crowds, sparked revival, and eventually landed him in prison. Bound by chains, John sent messengers to ask Jesus a question that revealed an inner struggle:

"Are you the one who is to come, or shall we look for another?" (Matthew 11:3). Can you feel his angst? The man who devoted his entire life to proclaiming Christ—and was about to die for his message—now wondered if it was all in vain.

Again, honest struggle collided with divine patience. Jesus returned John's messengers to the imprisoned prophet with a word of assurance. This would have been kindness enough—but what Jesus did next was astounding.

As the messengers walked away, Jesus turned to the crowds to *brag* about John. "Truly, I say to you, among those born of women there has arisen no one greater than John the Baptist" (Matthew 11:11). John received his highest commendation at his lowest point.

Now, it would be inaccurate to say that John was praised *because of* his doubt. But it's clear that his wrestling did not invalidate his faith in Jesus' eyes. If anything, his struggle served as a model for what Jesus says just a few verses later: "Come to me, all who labor and are heavy laden, and I will give you rest" (v 28). Even the greatest ministers are weighed down by uncertainty. And Jesus invites and commends those who bring him their burdened questions.

More wrestling was put on display when two sisters grappled with Jesus in their grief. We glanced at Mary's sorrow earlier. She and her sister, Martha, struggled with the Lord over their brother's death. Both brought him the same heartbroken lament: "Lord, if you had been here, my brother would not have died" (John 11:21, 32). This is simultaneously a statement of belief and complaint. They acknowledged Jesus' power but mourned his delay.

Though both sisters said the same thing, Jesus ministered to each of them uniquely. Martha needed to talk things through, so Jesus responded to her wrestling with words. Mary needed to cry things out, so Jesus responded to her weeping with tears. Both interactions show us that Christ welcomes the honest prayers of aching hearts.

Perhaps the most striking example of wrestling in Scripture is that which takes place in heaven. The last book of the Bible, Revelation, is adorned with episodes of epic worship. Voices surround God's throne to exalt his holiness, glory, and worth. But in the midst of all the praise, a refrain of pain arises. John describes the scene:

> I saw under the altar the souls of those who had been slain for the word of God and for the witness they had borne. They cried out with a loud voice, "O Sovereign Lord, holy and true, how long before you will judge and avenge our blood on those who dwell on the earth?"
>
> (Revelation 6:9-10)

This shocking picture shows martyrs lamenting—in heaven. Their prayer echoes the cry of every sufferer, "How long?" They call out to the Lord for justice and ask when he will finally vindicate their sacrifice. If God invites glorified saints to wrestle in heaven, surely he welcomes suffering saints to do so from earth.

In their book on prayer, J.I. Packer and Carolyn Nystrom compare God's view of honest wrestling with ours. They point out that neglecting to complain about hardship is typically viewed as a sign of strength, but Scripture shows us something different:

> *Yet we constantly find in the Bible that when bad things happen to good people, so that they feel totally at the end of their tether, they complain with great freedom and at considerable length to their God. And Scripture does not seem to regard these complaining prayers as anything other than wisdom.*[3]

So, to come back to the claim with which we started, since God is in control, is it up to us to question him? The surprising answer is, "yes." Of course, there are guardrails to our complaints, which we will discuss later on. But the Bible confounds us with a gracious God who welcomes our wrestling. Scripture tells the story of how God intervened in order to make a way for lost people to come into relationship with him. This is the gospel: that God's Son came into the world to die for our sins and rise on our behalf (1 Corinthians 15:3-5). Anyone who trusts in Jesus is not just forgiven, they're adopted (Romans 8:15). This change in status cannot be undone; if you're a Christian, you're a child of God. You can relate to him from a place of complete relational security (even in those seasons when it feels like you're barely holding onto faith). So your Father invites you to tell him when you struggle with his plan, timing, or apparent absence. When you do, you stand in the company of followers like Abraham, David, and Mary and Martha.

Those with strong faith bring God their questions and complaints.

When the time came for me to face God after those two silent months, I was "terrified at his presence" (Job 23:15). I knew he invited my honest wrestling, yet he had every right to humble me into submission. Fear gripped my soul—how would the Lord respond?

I shared my concerns with a friend who had recently been diagnosed with the cancer that would take his life. Mike reminded me of God's welcoming grace with a powerful image.

"No matter how hard you punch, Jesus' hands will stay at his side. He may 'touch your hip,' but God can, and does, humble himself to a punching bag."

Despite this advice, I still approached God with intensity and fear. I was ready for a fight, fully aware that I had no hope of prevailing. How did Jesus react to my wrestling? *He put down his hands.*

Indeed, he opened them: Jesus confronted me, not with condemnation, but compassion. Several passages, like the ones above, flooded my soul as I prayed. God heard me, held me, and hurt *with* me. My sadness did not disappear and my struggle was not done—but I knew my pain and heartache would not turn Christ away.

This is the place I pray you get to, as your sorrows rise and questions surface. Your weeping is not weak. Your wrestling is not wavering. And, as we're about to see, Jesus authorizes your groaning and joins you in your grief. So don't wipe away your tears or walk around your questions. Struggle faithfully.

CHAPTER 2

JESUS WEPT
AND WRESTLED

In the days after Eli's prenatal diagnosis, our hearts were chained to isolating fear and sorrow. It felt like no one would understand our agony. And no step forward seemed possible. How would we endure, as each day brought us closer to our son's death?

We turned to dear friends, desperate for help. Joel and Jen could have uttered a number of things that were true, but untimely. They could have lobbed platitudes at our pain. But they did very little talking. Instead, they listened through tears. And in the handful of words they did offer, one simple reminder whispered hope:

"Jesus knows what it's like."

This was no solution to our sorrow or spiritual reason for our suffering. It was an assurance that turned our tearful gaze to Christ. We were afraid. We were aching. But we were not alone. We were accompanied by one acquainted with agony. Jesus understood the depths of our despair. Jesus offered us solidarity in the storm. And Jesus would show us how to stagger forward in the darkness.

Have you ever felt like no one can understand what you're going through? The suffering you face may leave you feeling isolated and misunderstood. But whatever your sorrow, you have a Savior who knows your struggle. Anxiety, loneliness, depression, illness, fear, betrayal, abandonment, abuse, injustice, loss. *Jesus knows what it's like.*

But let me be clear: this is not a gospel-colored band-aid meant to be stretched over an open wound. It's not a trite tagline that sounds powerful but offers little for your pain. Rather, it's an invitation towards rugged hope for wounded believers. Jesus understands your suffering. He walks with you in the darkness. And he shows you how to endure—in a way that might surprise you.

In the last chapter we saw that some of the Bible's strongest believers wept and wrestled with God. But you may still have reservations: sure, stories of sorrowful saints might help us when we can't hold it together. But that doesn't necessarily mean they're intended as models to follow. They also sinned—yet we don't seek to imitate their immorality. So God may *allow* faithful struggle, but does he *encourage* it? As our maturity and faith increase, shouldn't our tears and questions decrease?

Let's consider how Jesus faced suffering. Believers are called to be "imitators of God" (Ephesians 5:1) and are being "conformed to the image of his Son" (Romans 8:29). So how did *perfect* faith encounter pain? Seeing how Jesus suffered will not only give you an example to follow, it will also show how he is your companion through any trial.

JESUS KNOWS WHAT IT'S LIKE TO WEEP

We have already heard Mary and Martha wrestle with the Lord over their brother's death. Yet if we return to that scene, we'll see how Jesus himself waded through grief.

Now when Mary came to where Jesus was and saw him, she fell at his feet, saying to him, "Lord, if you had been here, my brother would not have died." When Jesus saw her weeping, and the Jews who had come with her also weeping, he was deeply moved in his spirit and greatly troubled. And he said, "Where have you laid him?" They said to him, "Lord, come and see." Jesus wept. So the Jews said, "See how he loved him!" (John 11:32-36)

Do you see how Jesus expressed his feelings? He knows what it's like for emotions to rise to the surface in the presence of others. We often do our best to hold back tears even in the face of death—but Jesus let them flow.

What's most surprising about his weeping is how *unnecessary* it seems. He knew that the pain was about to be over—moments later he would raise Lazarus from the dead (v 43-44). If there was ever a time for dry eyes at a funeral, this was it. Jesus could have told everyone to stop crying. But he slowed down. He saw their tears. And he wept.

Why? Why waste time with misery before the miracle? One answer that the Bible gives us is because it's wise:

> *Sorrow is better than laughter,*
> *for by sadness of face the heart is made glad.*
> *The heart of the wise is in the house of mourning,*
> *but the heart of fools is in the house of mirth.*
> *(Ecclesiastes 7:3-4)*

Listen to what Ecclesiastes is saying. Sorrow is *better* than laughter. Mourning is the *wise* choice in death's wake. We tend to admire those who maintain a peaceful or positive disposition, even in grief. We're inclined to silence or to suppress sadness, thinking that engaging heartache will only deepen our despair. But Scripture confronts both of these misconceptions. The wise do not skip past grief to gladness. Rather, they know that grieving decongests the soul and opens it up to deeper joy, "for by sadness of face the heart is made glad." This is what Jesus displays at Lazarus' tomb. Wisdom weeps.

Another reason that Jesus shed tears was to showcase his love. John 11 makes it explicit that Jesus *loved* Mary and Martha (v 5). The late pastor Tim Keller put it well when he said that Jesus wept "because he's perfect love."[4] By crying, Christ displayed his compassion for these grieving sisters. He made their sorrow his own. Affection is affected by others' affliction. Love weeps with those who weep.

His tears also expressed his love for Lazarus. When the bystanders saw Jesus weeping, they said, "See how he loved him!" (v 36). They saw Jesus' heartache as honoring to his friend. Nicholas Wolterstorff, a contemporary theologian and bereaved father, makes a similar connection between tears and love when he writes, "Grief is existential testimony to the worth of the one loved . Every lament is a love song."[5] We mourn because people matter. Jesus knows what it's like to be occupied by someone else's absence. His tears testified to his loved one's worth.

Jesus didn't only cry on behalf of others—he also expressed sorrow over his own suffering. Before handing himself over to be crucified, he gathered with his disciples in the Garden of Gethsemane. There, he "began to be greatly distressed and troubled" (Mark 14:33). He confided in his closest friends, "My soul is very sorrowful, even to death" (v 34). Imminent death stifled him—and he wasn't embarrassed to show it. If you were in his position, would you want to show your friends confident composure? Yet Jesus' march towards crucifixion was no triumphant battle cry. He who holds all things together had no problem falling apart.

These portraits show why Jesus was called "a man of sorrows and acquainted with grief" (Isaiah 53:3). The one who "upholds the universe by the word of his power" (Hebrews 1:3) bent under the burdens of a broken world. His strength and sovereignty did not prevent him from giving full expression to his heartache. And he encouraged others to do the same—he preached what he practiced. He endorsed weeping as faithful by saying, "Blessed are those who mourn" (Matthew 5:4). Grief is not merely human, it's holy. Your tears do not display weakness. They make you more like your Savior.

And when the sadness that grips your soul also tries to convince you that no one understands your trouble, remember the solidarity of Jesus' tears. As the pastor Dane Ortlund says, "In our pain, Jesus is pained; in our suffering, he feels the suffering as his own."[6]

JESUS KNOWS WHAT IT'S LIKE TO WRESTLE

It probably wouldn't shock you to learn that Scripture describes Jesus' prayers as "reverent." What else would we expect from the Son of God? But it might surprise you to hear what his reverence sounded like. Listen to how Hebrews summarizes Jesus' prayer life: "In the days of his flesh, Jesus offered up prayers and supplications, with loud cries and tears, to him who was able to save him from death, and he was heard because of his reverence" (Hebrews 5:7). It's common to refer to one-on-one time with God as "quiet time." But while Jesus' devotionals were reverent, they were far from silent. They were *loud* and *tearful*.

And Hebrews tells us that this was not an occasional occurrence, but a description of his prayers "in the days of his flesh." That is, his whole life was marked by intense conversations with the Father. Maybe this is why he often retreated to the wilderness to pray (Luke 5:16)—not for some peace and quiet, but for space to make noise as he wrestled with his Father.

We see this on display in two particular scenes, the first taking us back to Gethsemane on the night before Jesus died. After disclosing his distress to his disciples, Jesus turned to prayer. You might expect him to have asked for strength to endure the torture that was about to occur. But Jesus didn't ask for a way *through*, he begged for a way *out*. Mark tells us that he "prayed that, if it were possible, the hour might pass from him" (Mark 14:35). He pleaded with the Father, "Remove this cup from me" (v 36). And this was not just a one-time appeal. He repeated this prayer *three times*. Jesus knows what it's like to anticipate suffering you'd rather avoid.

This prayer became ammunition for some of Christianity's earliest opponents. To the Roman mind it was unthinkable for sorrow to accompany strength. They mocked Jesus because a "virtuous person faced death with calm and courage, not with tears and fears."[7] It was ridiculous for God to suffer on behalf of sinners *willingly*. It was all the more ludicrous for him to suffer *tearfully*.

We, too, can struggle with this portrayal of Jesus. Our temptation is to gloss over his anguished plea to the Father and instead highlight his conclusion: "Yet not what I will, but what you will" (v 36). People encourage us to move toward the same resolve—to cultivate settled trust in God's will. Yet we rarely hear an equal endorsement to desperately plead for a different way.

But we should question our discomfort with Jesus' wrestling. Why do his prayers unsettle us? Maybe our picture of strength needs realignment. We saw this in several examples in the last chapter, and now we see it in Jesus: those who are strong can engage their hearts as they step forward in faith. Christ displayed true courage as he entrusted his entire soul to the Father. He was both trusting and troubled. And he shows us that yielding to the Father's will often requires honest wrestling. Submission comes through struggle.

Jesus' petitions also stretch our understanding of biblical contentment. You are probably familiar with Paul's example, who famously wrote from death-row: "I have learned in whatever situation I am to be content" (Philippians 4:11). It's easy to think that a peaceful posture like this requires that we welcome struggle without resistance. But contentment does not mean passive acceptance. Jesus (and Paul for that matter) shows us that it's okay to want suffering to end.[8] You are allowed to dislike your difficulties. And God invites your impassioned pleas for him to ease or erase your sorrow, according to his will. Contentment does not silence cries for change: it flows from them.

Jesus' wrestling didn't end in Gethsemane. His loud and tearful prayers continued to his final moments. Following his betrayal, arrest, mocking, and abuse, his cry from the cross thundered towards heaven: "My God, my God, why have you forsaken me?" (Matthew 27:46). The words came from the first line of David's lament in Psalm 22. He questioned his Father from the depths of greatest anguish.

The author Glenn Pemberton helps us understand Jesus' cross-bound cry:

[Jesus'] lament—his questioning of God's presence—was not the result of doubt or some lack of faith that came over him. Jesus knows the plan; he is aware of the resurrection in three days and the ascension to follow. But none of this knowledge changes the pain, the human sense of desperation, and the feeling of abandonment.[9]

Jesus knew the answer to his question, "Why?", yet he still cried out to the Father. Now, we can't overlook the uniqueness of Jesus' suffering—he died to consume the full cup of sin's punishment for our sake. But it's tempting to turn the crucifixion into a comparison. Under the cross's shadow our suffering can seem so insignificant. We will never taste such terror, so how could we ever cry out like Jesus?

But Jesus' sacrifice was never meant to silence our sorrow. For one thing, God had already established honest wrestling as a legitimate way to pray—generations of believers uttered Psalm 22 long before Christ did. Jesus' lament brought further validity to desperate questions and cries.

Second, if Jesus' suffering was meant to silence "lesser" laments, his ministry would have looked frightfully different. He would have met cries for mercy and healing with indifference and superiority. But Jesus never rolled his eyes when he helped the hurting. He never used his own anguish to trivialize others' trials. No, he was hospitable to heartache. His soul did not cringe with condescension, it overflowed with compassion.

Christ leaves no uncertainty: those who lament are full of faith. Jesus leads the procession of limping believers who wrestle honestly with God. He knows what it's like to struggle with the Father with pleas and questions.

LIKE JESUS

So how does *perfect* faith encounter pain? It weeps and it wrestles. Expressing your agony is not only allowed, it's encouraged. To be Christ-like and "walk in the same way in which he walked" (1 John 2:6) does not just apply to things like compassion, patience, and humility. It means that we will also grieve and groan like Jesus did. We can pray like he prayed—with loud cries and tears. As Pemberton says, "Let's not try to be less human than the Son of God."[10] You imitate your Savior when you weep and wrestle.

This challenges those of us who have learned to be skeptical of emotions. Phrases like "faith over feelings" or "trust God, not your emotions" can promote spiritual suspicion of anything sentimental. But Jesus does not pit truth against tears—he shows us that reverence and wrestling go hand in hand. So allow his heart to soften your faith to trust *and* feel. I hope that the pages ahead will help you do just that.

And if you have been the recipient of such suspicion, the loud cries and tears of Christ are your defense. Your sorrows and struggles are not a sign of deficient faith.

So when you encounter something sad, be sad. Let Jesus' tomb-side tears slow your soul to feel the sorrow. It's loving to lament. It's wise to grieve.

When you agonize in the darkness, think of Jesus' groans in Gethsemane. You do not need to feel guilty for wanting God to change the path ahead. It's okay to ask for a different way. Jesus' pleading permits your anguished requests.

And when you can't understand why God is allowing such agony, hear Christ's cry from the cross. Suffering can reduce your prayers down to one word: *Why?* Jesus punctuated his prayer with a question mark. You can, too.

WITH JESUS

Jesus invites us one step further. We don't only groan *like* Jesus, we groan *with* Jesus. That is, Jesus groans *with you*. His weeping and wrestling express his solidarity with you. Jesus does not scroll past your pain with indifference. He is your commiserating companion. Your sadness becomes his. When you weep, Jesus weeps. When you hurt, Jesus hurts. He is troubled by your troubles. His heart aches in rhythm with yours. He knows what it's like.

Nicholas Wolterstorff captured this in a prayer as he grieved the loss of his son. As he weeps and wrestles with the Lord, he turns his gaze to a weeping and wrestling Savior:

> *How is faith to endure, O God, when you allow all this scraping and tearing on us? You have allowed rivers of blood to flow, mountains of suffering to pile up, sobs to become humanity's song—all without lifting a finger that we could see. You have allowed bonds of love beyond number to be painfully snapped. If you have not abandoned us, explain yourself. We strain to hear. But instead of hearing an answer we catch sight of God himself scraped and torn. Through our tears we see the tears of God.*[11]

To see Jesus' tears will not necessarily ease the tension you face in suffering. It may even cause deeper confusion: the very one who weeps with you is the one you wrestle with. If he is so moved by your misery, why doesn't he just end it?

Spiritual slogans abound to answer that question, but none sufficiently resolve the dilemma. Instead, you may find yourself troubled in your own Gethsemane, fighting to trust the Lord. But your faithful decision to struggle honestly puts you in the company of the courageous. And God will wait for you patiently, listen to you tearfully, and sustain you graciously, even as your prayers to him end in exclamation points and question marks.

Learning of Eli's diagnosis introduced an agony that I had never thought possible. I didn't know what to do with my sorrow as I anticipated the loss of my son. But the tears of Jesus guided my grief as both a father and a husband.

As Eli's dad, I saw in Jesus' example that my weeping was not wasteful or weak. If the Son of God cried over loss and suffering, I did not need to feel ashamed of my mourning. His weeping at Lazarus' tomb taught me how grief can be a profound expression of love. I didn't have to suppress or rush my sadness, because my tears proclaimed my son's worth. I grieved—because Eli was a precious gift.

As Jillian's husband, I witnessed a staggering display of Christlike love and faith in her. Her own Gethsemane was facing the reality that she would continue the pregnancy, knowing it would end in devastation. Yet she graciously gave her body to carry and deliver our son at great cost to herself. Her fierce love for Eli never wavered as she cherished his life and mourned his eventual loss. And she did so with honest faith—struggling with the Father while fighting to trust him.

You, too, can step forward with honest faith. In the next chapter, we'll learn how to weep and wrestle faithfully like Jesus did.

CHAPTER 3

LEARNING
TO LAMENT

Tears dampened my Bible as our ministry team studied Psalm 43 together. The conversation slowed to a silence as they gave me a chance to gather my words. The ache inside me held a mixture of grief and gratitude. Here's why.

Psalms 42 and 43 form a two-part song written by a suffering worship leader. Tension pulses as he struggles with his sorrow and his God. Declaration and doubt, trust and tears, confidence and confusion—all these twist together to form a ballad of battered faith.

Our study of this song stirred up the grief that gripped my heart. At that point weeping over Eli was a daily occurrence, so it didn't take much to trigger my tears. But something else was happening in this moment. These psalms weren't just bringing my sorrow to the surface— they were also teaching me how to lament.

Prior to this point, prayer had often felt like it should be a cordial conversation marked by calm supplication and subdued trust. But how could I speak to God when I was struggling with *him*? What was I meant to do with my aches, questions, and complaints? How could I rely on the one I felt hurt by? The psalmist's lament was giving me answers. It was paving a path for me to wrestle with God in prayer. While suffering had disoriented my soul, this psalmist's struggle was guiding my groans with words of honest faith.

In this chapter I hope that you will make a similar discovery. In the first two chapters we saw that strong faith weeps and wrestles with the Lord. From Genesis to Revelation, God's people bring him their troubles, questions, and needs. But you may be wondering, "How do I actually do that?" So we now turn to the Psalms to understand how to engage the Lord through the process of lament.

The Psalms, as a whole, are meant to shape how we approach God—and the psalmists lament with great frequency and fluency (see Appendix A). While each lament is unique, they all contain similar elements of how to cry out to the Lord. So we're going to explore the four common rhythms of lament—pain, protest, petition, and (eventual) praise— through the lens of Psalms 42 – 43. To get the most out of this chapter, I recommend reading these psalms now and keeping your Bible open as we work through it. As you walk the same path as the psalmist, I trust that you will learn how to pray through pain with honesty and hope.

EXPLAINED PAIN

Lament begins with explaining our pain to the Lord. Psalms 42 – 43 are filled with vivid descriptions. The author begins by comparing himself to a panting deer:

As a deer pants for flowing streams,
  so pants my soul for you, O God.
My soul thirsts for God,
  for the living God.
When shall I come and appear before God?

(Psalm 42:1-2)

Common depictions of this prayer show a peaceful scene with a deer near a stream. But that is far from the setting of this psalm—a panting deer is a dying deer. Short breaths. Dry throat. Dangerous thirst. Desperation drives this prayer. The psalmist describes his experience with the Lord as thirst. In other words, God is a necessity that's absent. You might think that this thirst is affectionate longing, like fiancés awaiting their wedding day. But we will see that this prayer is not delightful romance. This is intimate conflict.

The psalmist goes on to explain that his spiritual emptiness is matched by desperate loneliness. He aches for joyful worship with God's people, but fellowship is a fading memory (v 4). Instead of enjoying the company of friends, he endures the contempt of foes (v 3, 10). He is far from Jerusalem, far from the temple, far from home (v 6).

This downcast castaway does not downplay his pain. His prayer is full of visceral details. Did the Lord know all these things already? Yes. But the psalmist prays as if God is unaware. He takes the Lord on a descriptive tour through his experience in the wilderness. And God walks along with an attentive ear.

Descriptive prayers like this occur all throughout Scripture. Believers take the time to slow down and describe their suffering to God, often in the present tense. Though God is all-knowing, and God's people know he is all-knowing, they still find the need to explain to him both their trouble and how they feel about it.[12]

In my experience, pain-filled explanations in prayer are rare among Christians. Why spend time informing God of things he already knows? Instead, our suffering prayers mainly consist of requests for things like comfort, healing, and strength. Yet the Lord also wants to hear us talk to him about our struggles.

Authors J. Alasdair Groves and Winston T. Smith capture the surprise of this invitation.

> *This is really quite a shocking thing for God to invite and even command us to do ... Yet this is exactly what we observe over and over in the Psalms. Too often, even taking the time to ask in prayer for God to help us or do things for us feels inconvenient and impractical. How much more inefficient, we think to ourselves, to do nothing but blabber on in prayer about one's feelings!*

Yet, in his mercy, God chooses to offer his listening ear to us, drawing out the depths of our soul in the safety of relationship with him.[13]

It may feel uncomfortable or unnecessary to describe your experiences and emotions to the Lord. But grace has purchased you a friendship with a listening God who encourages you to explain your pain.

Talking to God about your pain won't necessarily be easy— it first requires that you engage with what's going on in your soul, which takes courage. Confronting the darkness in you and around you is hard. And you're surrounded by distractions that disengage you from your heart. But to lament is a bold decision to linger on the difficulties you face. So be brave. Slow down. Seek to understand the brokenness you feel, and express it to God.

As the psalmists explain their pain, they do so with surprising creativity. Did you notice that Psalms 42 – 43 are colored with figurative language? "As a *deer* ... my soul *pants* ... tears have been my *food* ... I *pour out* my soul..." The author took the time to understand his pain and then help others imagine it. Engaging his emotions enabled him to articulate them with provocative precision.

Creative explanations like these may seem exaggerated. Did the psalmist really *eat* his tears? Probably not. It's more likely that he is describing the common experience of losing your appetite in grief. And when you weep for extended periods of time, the warm and salty tears find their way down your cheeks to your lips. "Tears for food" is a powerful image. It's not an overstatement, it's an illustration. Scripture encourages passionate and dramatic expression in prayer.

Of course, lament also allows for plain language. One lamenter says, "You hold my eyelids open" (Psalm 77:4), but another simply tells the Lord, "I lie awake" (102:7). It may not resonate to pray something like "I am a worm and not a man" (22:6). Perhaps you'd prefer just to say, "I am helpless" (88:15). Some might pray that their "eye is wasted from grief," (31:9) or you could just say, "to you, O LORD, I cry" (30:8). Whether it's a poignant illustration or a simple description, God encourages you to put your hurts into words.

When I talk about my grief, I'm tempted to use phrases like, "it's hard to explain," or "words can't describe." The limits of language can make it hard to articulate sorrow. But the Lord gave us lament so that our heartache can be heard. Suffering is indeed difficult to describe—but don't let that keep you from explaining your pain, as best as you can.

EXPRESSED PROTEST

Lament doesn't need to stop at explaining your pain to God—you're also invited to protest against it. I mentioned earlier that Psalms 42 – 43 are sometimes depicted as serene. You might get that impression from the psalmist's thirst (42:1-2) and recollection of God (v 6). But a closer look reveals deep conflict between this man and the

Lord—from the psalmist's perspective, at least. Confident declarations are quickly overtaken by difficult questions:

I say to God, my rock: "Why have you forgotten me?"
(Psalm 42:9)

For you are the God in whom I take refuge; why have you rejected me? (Psalm 43:2)

Do you feel the tension? In the same breath the psalmist appears to contradict his own affirmations. God is a *rock*, a source of stability and security—yet the Lord seems to have forgotten him. God is a *refuge*, a place of protection and peace—yet the Lord seems to have turned his loved one away. The psalmist questions the very things he confesses to be true about the Lord. His prayer is, essentially, "God, this is not who I know you to be."

You have likely experienced a disconnect between God's promises and your pain. Or perhaps you have witnessed injustice or disaster and wondered why the Lord allows such things to occur. *But who are we to protest our situation before a holy God?* you may have thought. *Who are we to complain to an infinite Creator from our limited perspective?* Yet that's exactly what he invites us to do. Biblical lament permits you to express your displeasure to God and ask him your difficult questions.

The Psalms regularly call out with candor. One sufferer cries, "Why do you hide yourself in times of trouble?" (10:1). Another asserts that God is so disinterested in his pain that the Lord must be taking a nap, "Awake! Why are you sleeping, O Lord?" (44:23). David asks, "How long, O LORD? Will you forget me forever?" (13:1) He says elsewhere, "Evening and morning and at noon, I utter my complaint and moan, and he hears my voice" (55:17). Yet another psalmist looks around at the injustice and asks, "O LORD, how long shall the wicked, how long shall the wicked exult?" (94:3).

These laments may seem to cross the line. But, as the author Glenn Pemberton explains, such honest prayers honor the Lord:

> [The psalmists] do not lack fear of God; it is because of their reverence and their relationship with God that they dare not engage in half-truths, dance around hidden thoughts, or suppress their feelings. They know that God will not stand for two-faced flattery. For these psalmists, either God is an intimate friend to whom we speak our true thoughts and feelings, or God, in fact, is no friend at all.[14]

The Psalms are the words God gave us to give back to him. So, far from being irreverent, protests like these are faithful ways to pray.

But protesting is not just a process to get things off your chest. Biblical lament shows us that complaints and questions are an avenue to intimacy. Rich and dynamic relationships do not avoid conflict. Rather, they deal with conflict in healthy ways. Lament allows you to do just that with the Lord. To be clear, when I speak of "conflict" with God, it's not two-way warfare. You may well be angry with God—but if you're in Christ, God is in no way angry with you (Romans 8:1). Instead, God patiently invites you to work through your struggles and wrestle for deeper unity with him. That's why the writer of Psalms 42 – 43 can ask God, "Why have you rejected me?" (v 2) and just a few sentences later say that the Lord is his "exceeding joy" (v 4). Voicing his protest has led to renewed intimacy. As the author Lindsay Wilson explains, "God will not be shattered or provoked by strong words of protest. God does not, unlike many of us, avoid conflict, for he knows that the honest expression of our current situation is essential for our transformation."[15]

You may be tempted to hide your frustration with God and pretend like everything's fine. (This could be rooted in a good desire to avoid grumbling, which we'll discuss in the next chapter.) Or you might be tempted to sever your relationship with God altogether, thinking that separation from the Lord will bring you the relief you need. But you don't have to choose between silence and separation. Lament offers you a third way. Honest worshipers resolve to work through their issues with the Lord. It might be a painful, messy, and lengthy process. But engaging in lament says we're not going anywhere—and neither is God.

Instead of protesting, however, I find that many Christians are quick to make declarations of trust in the face of difficulty. We push away doubt or wrestling and rush to proclaim promises over the pain. You can hear it in our prayers. "God, this is difficult, *but we know you're in control."* You can hear it in our songs. "It is well with my soul." You can hear it when we tag the end of hard news with, *"... but God is good."*

Let me be clear—it's not wrong to declare God's promises in the storm. Sufferers in Scripture do this over and over again. But they do not skip the necessary process of wrestling with the Lord.

Lament is God's invitation to be honest: you do not need to silence your questions for the sake of sounding more spiritual. The Lord commends your protests as faithful participation in a fractured world. There is probably suffering in your life that has not sat well with you. And there are plenty of tragedies in your community or news feed that should provoke your soul. So protest. Ask God your questions. Bring him your complaints.

EARNEST PETITION

Lament also positions you to bring God your earnest petitions.

A shift occurs from Psalm 42 to Psalm 43. The psalmist's pain and protests turn toward petition as he begs the Lord to act. He cries out, "Vindicate me ... defend my cause ... deliver me!" (Psalm 43:1). His urgent pleas come before the only one who can save. As we discussed, this change of tone does not erase his discomfort. These three petitions are followed by lingering questions in the next verse: "Why have you rejected me? Why do I go about mourning?" (v 2). His wrestling continues, yet he still asks for God's help:

Send out your light and your truth,
  let them lead me;
let them bring me to your holy hill
  and to your dwelling! (Psalm 43:3)

The psalmist goes to the only source he can for help. He knows only God can deliver him from danger and bring him through the darkness. His pain and protest culminate in a petition for God to bring him home.

Petition seems to be the aspect of lament that comes most naturally to many of us. We often ask God for help and comfort in times of need. But the Psalms broaden our understanding of requests by offering a variety of postures from which these petitions are made.

Sometimes lamenters call on God with boldness. They confidently cry out to the Lord, expecting him to show up (35:23). Other petitions come from a place of weariness, desperately asking God to listen or come close (22:11). Their trembling requests are their last resort. Still others make requests before their conflict with God has been resolved (90:13). They are wrestling with God, yet they still ask for his help. These different approaches demonstrate that what we ask God for, and how we ask him, can vary between people and situations.

After learning Eli's diagnosis, the prayers others made for us often added to our disorientation. Many were convinced that God would heal our son. Of course, we longed for the Lord to rescue Eli. But their expectation made it seem as though asking for a miracle was the only faith-filled and loving way to pray. Others confidently asked God to act according to his goodness and perfect plan. Their unwavering trust made us feel like we needed to resolve our sense of conflict with God before we could request his help. We didn't think that people were wrong for praying with confidence. And we are incredibly grateful for how they went to the Lord on our behalf. But it felt impossible to share their assurance or agree completely with their requests. We were still wrestling with God and didn't know what to ask for.

These stances of prayer seemed incompatible with one another. But the various petitions in the Psalms show that there are diverse ways to pray faithfully in the midst of pain. Sometimes assurance saturates your supplications. Other times, despair dilutes the confidence of your appeals. On other occasions your requests will rise before your conflict with God has resolved. The point is this: whether you are confident or crushed, the Lord is listening when you ask.

So what can you ask God for? You can plead with him to change the specifics of your circumstances. You can beg him to miraculously intervene. You can ask God to *please just do something*. And it's okay if you don't know what petitions to make. Scripture affirms that suffering can disorient our requests, but God has given us a translator: "For we do not know what to pray for as we ought, but the Spirit himself intercedes for us with groanings too deep for words" (Romans 8:26).

And when God doesn't answer your petitions in the way you pleaded for, your prayer becomes a lament for unanswered prayers. You can return to the Lord with a new lament, this time sharing with him your hurt over his previous response.

EVENTUAL PRAISE

A close look at Psalms 42 – 43 reveals a surprise ending— the prayer doesn't result in praise. It only *anticipates* praise. Look at the verb tenses: "*I shall again* praise him..." (43:5, my emphasis) "*Then I will* go to the altar of God ... *I will* praise you with the lyre" (v 4, my emphasis). This vow to praise is common in many laments. Praise is a future expectation, but not a present reality. The psalmist urges his soul to have hope but does not force himself to sing happily.

This lack of praise is all the more significant when we remember that this psalm is a worship song, composed for "the choirmaster" and written by a popular band of the day, "the Sons of Korah." Don't skip past the importance of this: even when praise is absent, worship can still occur. Sometimes trials can rob your ability to sing triumphantly. When sorrow grips your soul, or suffering lingers, you may feel pressured to push down your pain with praise, because that's what "good Christians" do. But lament enables you to engage the Lord—to weep, to wrestle, to *worship*— even when praise feels far away. Your heartache does not dishonor God. And you can, like the psalmist, share your pain honestly while you urge your soul to "hope in God" (v 5) waiting for the day when you will praise him again.

And while lament allows for times of praiseless worship, it also assures us that these seasons won't last forever. The Bible shows that voicing your sorrows and struggles can renew your trust and joy. Lament *enables* praise. This explicit shift is often seen in a lamenter's decision to praise God now, despite the surrounding distress. You can see this with words like "yet," "but," or "nevertheless." Suffering believers fight to trust the Lord in their trials, recalling his grace and mercy. Their pain gives way to praise. The book of Psalms as a whole follows a similar pattern. The psalms of lament are mostly concentrated at the beginning and middle of the book—but the praise builds to end with five poems of overflowing joy (Psalms 146 – 150). As Robert Smith says, "the singing of grief leads to the strengthening of hope."[16]

So whether praise feels far away or you're fighting for it now, lean into the process of lament to get you there. As you carry your pain, don't let go of God's promises. Hold the reality of your suffering alongside the truth of his steadfast love. Even when the tension has not resolved, rehearse what God has done and said he will do. Recount what you know to be true about the Lord. Your questions may not be answered, your circumstances may not change, and your grief may continue—but wrestling enables resilience. Brave the night with honest worship. Dawn is coming.

I trust that lament will pull you towards hope as you wrestle honestly with the Lord. And while these four rhythms can give shape to your prayers, they're not meant to be rigid or formulaic. The psalmists did not treat pain, protest, petition, and praise as a four-step process. Rather, they employed each aspect in varying degrees, depending on their circumstance. The lines are not always clear between each element, nor is there a fixed order to follow.[17] Praying about your suffering is not a linear path. Your laments will likely twist and turn with the complexity of what you face.

Here's a glimpse of how that looked for me. I penned several prayers as I anticipated Eli's birth and grieved his death. The first prayer I wrote down was the moment I mentioned in chapter 1. When I broke my two-month silence with God, I did so with words of protest and pain:

> *Why?*
> *O God, why?*
> *Why do you take him from me?*
> *Why?*
> *I'm so sad. I want Eli so bad.*
> *I want to be happy.*
> *I want Jillian to be happy.*
> *It's not well with my soul.*

Several months later, words of protest mingled with petition:

Where are you?
Come close.
You promise to listen.
So I'm talking.
You promise to heal, deliver, restore.
So I'm waiting.
Do something.
Please.

And the praise came eventually—a year and a half after Eli died. Tearful joy filled my soul. I wasn't done wrestling or grieving. But as the pain continued, my relational tension with the Lord had finally resolved:

I complain and rejoice.
The praise does not erase the pain.
But the pain no longer prevents the praise.

The time between these fragmented cries was filled with whispered prayers, countless tears, and frequent silence. But when I could put words to my hurt or pen to paper, lament led me. And I hope it will guide your groaning as well.

CHAPTER 4

GROANING WITHOUT GRUMBLING

I don't know how he did it. During my darkest days, Joel sat with me week in and week out. He asked thoughtful questions, listened to my sorrow, and watched countless tears fall. It was no easy task to accompany a new father awaiting the death of his firstborn. But Joel shouldered my burdens and helped me stumble toward the Lord.

He says it was a privilege to be entrusted with my tears—and that it was incredibly difficult. My agony was raw. And some things I said concerned him. A few of my theological questions and ways I interacted with Scripture raised his eyebrow. *Should I say something?* he wondered.

What Joel faced is a common dilemma. How far is too far in lament? When does faithful groaning cross the line into sin? Perhaps this is a tension you feel as you suffer, or as you support someone who does. You appreciate God's invitation to wrestle honestly, but you don't want to be a pessimist, cynic, or whiner. To put it in biblical terms, you don't want to *grumble*. After all, the Bible says to "do all things without grumbling" (Philippians 2:14) and names it at the top of a list of ungodliness (Jude 1:16). Lament and grumbling sound awfully similar, so wouldn't it be safer to just avoid both and count your blessings instead?

Your hesitation is likely rooted in a genuine desire to honor the Lord. But many believers misunderstand what grumbling is, leading them to avoid God's invitation to find robust hope through faithful groaning. In this chapter, we're going to explore the difference between grumbling and lament. Understanding this will liberate you to lament with confidence. Your honest prayers will not incur God's condemnation. Rather than tiptoeing through lament, or avoiding it altogether, you can groan boldly because of God's grace.

THE SIN OF GRUMBLING

Grumbling is often used interchangeably with "complaining," causing significant confusion. Many believers think it's sinful to speak negatively about their difficulties. But despite what you may have read or heard, complaining is not always a sin. As we've already seen, godly people complain to the Lord all throughout the Bible, including the Psalms.[18] And if the Psalms are the words that God gave us to give back to him, it can't be inherently wrong to complain.

In Psalm 142, David defines what it means to complain: "I pour out my complaint before him; I tell my trouble before him" (v 2). According to this verse, to complain is simply to tell your trouble. Harold Senkbeil compares it to something we're all familiar with:

> *When you go to your doctor, you're not whining; you're just explaining where you hurt. You list your complaints because you know your condition should receive attention. It may not go away; some of the symptoms may remain. But you've gone to someone who can do something about it.*[19]

Similarly, we can complain in a God-honoring way. That's what lament is—telling our troubles to God. So when it comes to grumbling, complaining is not the problem. The issue is *how* we complain. Lament involves *faithful* complaint; grumbling involves *sinful* complaint.

What, then, makes grumbling sinful? Numbers 14 provides an answer. God had rescued Israel from Egyptian captivity, carried them through the wilderness, and was about to deliver them into the promised land. But a frightening report of nearby enemies instilled in them significant doubt. God's people responded with grumbling:

> *Then all the congregation raised a loud cry, and the people wept that night. And all the people of Israel grumbled against Moses and Aaron. The whole congregation said to them, "Would that we had died in the land of Egypt! Or would that we had died in this wilderness! Why is the LORD bringing us into this land, to fall by the sword? Our*

wives and our little ones will become a prey. Would it not be better for us to go back to Egypt?" And they said to one another, "Let us choose a leader and go back to Egypt."

(Numbers 14:1-4)

Do you hear how similar this sounds to lament? Israel raised a loud cry and wept—the same description used of Jesus' prayers (Hebrews 5:7). The threat of enemies caused them to call out, "why?" just like in many psalms. And Israel despaired of life and struggled with God's plan, just as the psalmists did. Yet, this complaint in Numbers 14 is the sort of grumbling that the Lord forbids. When we read on, we discover that because of their grumbling, God kept this generation of Israelites out of the promised land (Numbers 14:22-23). So how is this incident so different from faithful groaning?

The crucial difference is this: grumblers don't care about working things out with the Lord. Three aspects of Israel's grumbling clue us into this.

You first see this in *who* Israel complained to. They spoke to Moses and Aaron, they spoke to each other, but they never complained to God. In this way, grumbling is similar to gossip. You talk *about* the person but never speak *to* them. As we see in the Psalms, God invites his peoples' complaints. But grumblers don't engage the Lord. That's not to say that you can't tell others about your problems or difficulties with God. But to never bring your troubles to the Lord is the way of grumbling.

Second, you see the difference in what Israel *did* with their complaints—they never moved past them. Numbers 14 is just one episode in a long season of grumbling where they *only* complained. Grumblers let themselves stay in a cycle of perpetual complaint. Lamenters, on the other hand, fight to move beyond their pain and protest toward petition and praise. It may take time, but they endeavor to process their complaints before God and wrestle towards trust in him.

Finally, you see the *trajectory* of grumblers' complaints. Instead of struggling with the Lord, Israel concludes, "Let us choose a leader and go back to Egypt" (v 4). Consider the gravity of their statement. The exodus was the ultimate event of redemption in the Old Testament. So Israel's choice to return to Egypt was not simply a desire for an easier life—they were essentially saying that God's salvation was irrelevant, their freedom no longer mattered, and they did not want to be God's people anymore. They rejected the Lord's grace, rescue, and provision. They decided that he was cruel. Then, they turned around. Grumbling and lament both struggle with God's promises, but lamenters keep wrestling. Grumblers walk away.

Lamenting and grumbling sound similar at the outset. You could cut most of Numbers 14 and paste it into several lament psalms without drawing too much attention. Both use strong language. Both convey visceral emotion. Both ask hard questions. Both struggle with God's presence, promises, and plan.

Where they diverge is in their posture toward the Lord. Lamenters move toward God in their wrestling. Their trajectory is trust. But grumblers don't ever move beyond their pain or protests. They don't work out their troubles with the Lord—they let their troubles turn them away. Their complaints become conclusions. This is why the Bible often associates grumbling with idolatry, rebellion, and unbelief.[20] The direction of grumbling is relational rejection, a "stubborn refusal to trust God's promises."[21]

Knowing this about grumbling ought to encourage you. If you are suffering right now, or you're still processing past hurts and trauma, the fact that you're reading this book is probably evidence that you're still holding on to the Lord—or rather, that he's still holding on to you. You may be struggling with his promises. His plan might feel harsh. Your eyes may have even glanced back at Egypt. But you have not yet concluded that the Lord is cruel. You haven't walked away. So keep fighting the temptation to turn your back on God.

And if you're walking alongside someone who is struggling, be slow to label them as a grumbler. Wrestling with the Lord takes time. So walk with them patiently and help them bring their complaints to the Lord.

THE SOLUTION OF LAMENT

Grumbling is often misdiagnosed—we assume that all complaining is sinful. It's also misprescribed—we fight it with the wrong remedy. Namely, we try to battle grumbling with gratitude. We are, indeed, called to "give thanks in all circumstances" (1 Thessalonians 5:18). But we're not meant to offer gratitude to the exclusion of our groans. And thankfulness alone will not automatically solve the issue. For example, if there's disagreement and tension between friends, simply focusing on the positives will not bring about resolution. Even the grumbling Israelites thanked the Lord and "flattered him with their mouths" (Psalm 78:36). But their praise stayed on the surface of their hearts and evaporated quickly.

The Bible offers a more formidable antidote.

Sufferers in Scripture don't just find the silver lining in the storm. The psalmists don't only count their blessings. Jesus doesn't play the thankful game from the cross. They all *lament*. Their groaning guards them from grumbling, gives voice to their grief, and results in gratitude and trust.

In contrast to grumbling, lament allows you to maintain your relationship with God even when you want to walk away. You may feel that God is being unloving or unmerciful. But instead of turning those feelings into a conclusion, lament helps you turn them into a conversation. To continue talking to the Lord is to continue walking with him.

So does this mean that, as long as we're talking *to* God, anything goes? No. Scripture cautions us: "Be not rash with your mouth, nor let your heart be hasty to utter a word before God, for God is in heaven and you are on earth. Therefore, let your words be few" (Ecclesiastes 5:2). Our words matter, especially when we're trying to work things out with someone. How much more so with the Lord?

But this warning makes the strong language of lament stand out all the more. Think about how brash some psalms are. Even though God "will not slumber" (Psalm 121:3), lamenters ask the Lord why he's sleeping while they suffer (44:23). God may "[give] to his beloved sleep," (127:2) but one sufferer cries out to him, "You hold my eyelids open" (77:4). One psalmist declares, "Your right hand upholds me" (63:8). Yet another asks the Lord why he keeps his hands in his pockets as his people suffer (74:11). And though David acknowledges that there's nowhere he can go from God's presence (139:7-12), he also asks why the Lord has abandoned him, forsaken him, and turned his face away (13:1; 22:1). You might assume that these impassioned words were hastily uttered before the Lord. But they were carefully crafted and became prayers God wants his people to repeat. The psalmists found ways to complain without diluting their pain *and* without dishonoring their God. They knew that, while the Lord forbids disrespect, he also welcomes directness.

Lament enables you to honor the Lord *and* be honest. Just as spouses or friends can respectfully share how they've been hurt by the other, you can also bring your complaints to God without giving way to hostility or contempt.

One way to put this into practice is to write out your laments. You might think this removes the authenticity of your conversations with God. But the reason we can read any prayer in the Bible is because someone wrote them down. Putting your pain onto paper can help you engage and articulate what's going on in your heart without being hasty. Write out your pain, your protest, your petition, and your praise.

But whether you write out your laments or not, fight against sinful grumbling with faithful complaining. Tell your troubles to the Lord.

THE SAFETY OF GRACE

But what if you get it wrong? What if you go too far? What if you *are* hasty with your words before the Lord? The book of James offers a surprising answer.

After James warns believers not to "grumble against one another," he highlights Job as an example of steadfastness (James 5:9-11). If you're familiar with Job's story, this may come as a surprise. Job deeply loved the Lord and endured excruciating loss, but he also made a lot of questionable statements. Yet James says that following Job's footsteps will put you on a different path than grumblers. Let's see why.

Job experienced the unimaginable: losing his wealth, home, health, and children. And those closest to him deepened his despair. His wife told him to curse God (Job 2:9) and his so-called friends were "miserable comforters" (16:2). The following snapshot gives you a taste of his turmoil:

God gives me up to the ungodly
  and casts me into the hands of the wicked.
I was at ease, and he broke me apart;
  he seized me by the neck and dashed me to pieces;
he set me up as his target;
  his archers surround me.
He slashes open my kidneys and does not spare;
    he pours out my gall on the ground. (Job 16:11-13)

All throughout the book Job's prayers twist and turn. In one moment he claims the Lord "mocks at the calamity of the innocent" (9:23), in another he cries out "my Redeemer lives" (19:25). He swings between rugged confidence and intense confrontation: "Though he slay me, I will hope in him; yet I will argue my ways to his face" (13:15). His faith shakes with honesty.

Do you ever have conflicting thoughts and feelings about God? For example, you believe that God is in control, but sometimes the chaos around you seems to indicate otherwise. Like Job, you stake your hope in your Redeemer but can't fathom why he would allow such heartache. When these conflicts occur in our hearts, we can fear coming across as a grumbler. So we're quick to reconcile these apparent contradictions with theological truth and reason.

But Job's story doesn't rush us to spiritual solutions. The sheer length of the book requires that we listen patiently to Job's honest wrestling. And his "friends" show us that formulaic faith is cold and empty. As Christopher Ash says,

Job shows us that "there is no instantaneous working through grief, no quick fix to pain."[22] God knows that faith in suffering is exhausting and complex. He relieves you of the pressure to tie up your sorrow in tidy truth.

The twists and turns of Job's wrestling regularly come back to the same cry: his repeated insistence that the Lord answer him. And after 37 dense and grueling chapters, God finally responds—with a surprising answer. He both challenges *and* accepts Job's wrestling.

After reading Job's critiques and accusations, most people don't have trouble seeing why God challenges him. The Lord speaks powerfully for four chapters, leading Job to "repent in dust and ashes" (42:1-6) for speaking of things beyond his comprehension. If the story stopped there, our takeaway might be to simply trust God in any trial and tread carefully with our words. But the next verse frustrates such a conclusion.

The Lord also *accepts* Job's wrestling. You see this in how God scolds Job's friends: "My anger burns against you … for you have not spoken of me what is right, as my servant Job has" (42:7). Don't gloss over God's assessment: Job spoke *rightly* about the Lord. How could God now approve of Job's words? Sure, he made profound statements of trust in the midst of paralyzing trials. But his imprecise theology and combative tone hardly seem acceptable. Yet the Lord validates his servant, Job.

Two reasons for God's approval rise to the surface.

The first is Job's *posture*. Though he prayed with an edge at times, he kept turning to the Lord. Unlike the grumbling Israelites, who had no interest in working things out with God, Job kept engaging the Lord. His complaints never became conclusions. Even as he felt that God had turned against him and tormented him for no reason, Job longed "to bring his perplexity to God himself."[23] He wept. He wrestled. He waited. And he refused to walk away.

But we can't ignore the fact that Job crossed the line, as evidenced by his repentance. Which leads to the second, and more important, aspect of the Lord's approval. *God's acceptance of Job proclaims his grace.* According to James, Job's story shows that "the Lord is compassionate and merciful" (James 5:11). He is patient with those who are in pain. As Derek Kidner says, "God knows the difference between struggling faith and contemptuous unbelief."[24]

The line between grumbling and lament may seem thin at times. But your task in suffering's storm is not perfect navigation. Rather, you are called to keep stumbling toward the God of grace.

Knowing that Eli would not come home with us was excruciating. But our nightmare got worse. Labor began ten weeks early, tearing him away far sooner than we feared. Our fragile plans to create memories with him were crushed. Had delivery occurred just days later, we would have had pictures with him from a maternity shoot and a photo session with my entire family. The photographs we longed for were never taken. We also ached to celebrate Christmas while Jillian was pregnant with him, as his due date was January 12. But early labor meant that every holiday season now reminds us of the only Christmas we never got to share with our firstborn. And we had agonized over a dedication service that was supposed to happen that Sunday. But before we could dedicate him with family and friends, Eli was no longer with us.

This torrent of sorrow culminated in one unanswered prayer: one minute. My earnest petition was begging God for *one minute* with Eli alive. Just one minute so we could hear his cries and hold him while he breathed his only breaths. Other babies with Eli's condition can live for hours or days, so it seemed like a small request for the one who spoke creation into existence. But Eli was born without breath. And that silence still echoes in my soul.

The timing of Eli's birth, under God's sovereign hand, seemed calculated and cruel. Like Job, I felt as though the Lord had "seized me by the neck and dashed me to pieces" (Job 16:12). I, too, wanted to "argue my ways to his face" (13:15). Why did he allow things to get worse when we were stepping out in faith to honor him and our son? Why didn't he let us have a mere minute with our dying child?

This led to the wrestling that made my friend, Joel, wonder whether or not he should speak up. He could have been like Job's friends and answered my questions with cold theology or pointed out which grievances sounded like grumbling. Instead, he decided to keep listening. This isn't because Joel fears challenging me. On the contrary, he's been one of my most faithful confronters over the years. Yet he sensed that even in my most visceral moments I was moving toward the Lord, not away. So he wept with me as I wrestled and gently turned my eyes to Christ. His patient companionship kept me from turning my back on God. And he helped me see how Jesus held onto me.

Suffering may cause you to entertain dark questions about the Lord. You might even say foolish things that you will one day regret and repent of. But God's compassion does not depend on your ability to struggle perfectly. Fight against grumbling by continuing to turn to the Lord. Bring him your complaints, your sorrows, your questions—and he will embrace you with empathy. Wrestle with him through pain, protest, petition, and praise. Tell your trouble to God. And if you cross the line, remember the cross. God covers your groans in grace.

CHAPTER 5

SORROWFUL YET REJOICING

Soon after Jillian told me she was pregnant, I began dreaming about the future with our firstborn. The color of his nursery, the commotion in our home, the privilege of parenting—all the expected changes, both small and major, came with much anticipation. One dream that began to stir my excitement was our eventual bedtime routine. When I was young, my mom often sang hymns at my bedside. I wanted to do the same for my son. A ukulele seemed like a fitting addition, so I planned to buy one by the time he arrived.

But when we found out that Eli would not come home with us from the hospital, this bedtime routine was added to the long list of ambushed dreams. And the prospect of his inevitable loss took away my capacity for singing.

My inability to lift my voice felt glaringly obvious the first time we went back to church after the diagnosis. The congregation sang—I stood there and wept. Their praise pierced our hearts as everyone cried out, "O, death, where is your sting?" My soul answered their rhetorical question: *it's right here.* Those around us sang triumphantly, but death had left us silent.

In the midst of our despair, Jillian's aunt graciously countered our songless sorrow. Terry, who knew great loss herself, offered us a promise that felt impossible to believe. Knowing nothing of my dashed desire to sing to Eli, Terry looked into our eyes with gentle confidence and said, "Your hearts will sing again."

Her words hurt with hope. We longed for them to be true, but the storm had only just started to rage. Each day brought us closer to Eli's grave—how could our hearts ever sing again? I knew Scripture's call to "count it all joy" (James 1:2) and "rejoice in our sufferings" (Romans 5:3), but I now questioned my understanding of these passages. Or maybe I was simply incapable of carrying them out. Either way, my faith felt deficient. And the road ahead seemed to conceal any possibility of joy.

Suffering can sometimes make joy feel unattainable. If you have been there, I hope you know by now that you're not alone. We've seen several examples of suffering saints in Scripture who wondered if their hearts would sing again. But I haven't met many people who wish to stay sorrowful forever. Lament may seem like a good option for those who are content with their sadness, but what if you *want* to feel happy? Won't engaging your agony only deepen your despair? And doesn't the Bible command us to rejoice in *all* circumstances? These questions can drive us to think that focusing on the positive is the only way to find joy in pain.

But lament and rejoicing are not opposed to one another. In this chapter, we're going to address this collision between joy and sorrow. We'll see that not only can they dwell together, but they can also work together to produce honest and hopeful faith.

JOY CAN OCCUR *WITH* SORROW

We tend to think of sorrow and joy as opposite emotions. So when we hear Scripture's instructions to rejoice in suffering, we can assume that it's at the exclusion of sadness. But the Bible does not put joy and sorrow at odds. While there are occasions in which each emotion may take center stage, they're not supposed to repel each other. They can both be present at the same time.

The apostle Paul put this on display. At first glance, it may seem that he made little space for sorrow. He faced intense suffering with abundant rejoicing: "In all our affliction, I am overflowing with joy" (2 Corinthians 7:4). And this was not just his own demeanor. He regularly told believers to rejoice, regardless of their situation: "Rejoice always, pray without ceasing, give thanks in all circumstances" (1 Thessalonians 5:16-18). It can seem that Paul's expectation for Christians was to be, as one old hymn goes, "happy all the day."[25]

But a closer look shows that Paul did not simply navigate life with a sunny disposition. Rather, his faith held room for both darkness and light, much like when the moon blocks the sun in a solar eclipse. When this happens, it's as if night and day occur simultaneously. You can't deny that the sun still shines, but you also can't disregard the darkness. Similarly, Paul did not forget the hope of God's promises, nor did he ignore the hardships of suffering. He recognized both at the same time.

You see examples of this in his letter to the Romans. Paul remembers the light as he says, "We rejoice in our sufferings" (Romans 5:3). He also grieves the darkness when he says that suffering makes us "groan inwardly" (8:23). Rejoicing and groaning do not contradict each other. They can coexist.

He goes on to speak of his "great sorrow and unceasing anguish" (9:2) as he considers his relatives who don't know Jesus. Think about that. Paul, who encouraged others to rejoice *always*, also had *unceasing* anguish in his heart.[26] Joy and sorrow were not alternating visitors to Paul's life. They both took up permanent residence in his soul. Faith intermingles joy and sorrow.

And this mingling is not unique to Paul—joy occurs alongside sorrow all throughout Scripture. In one psalm, David spoke of "sorrow in [his] heart all the day" (Psalm 13:2) and then said his "heart shall rejoice" (v 5). The wise man of Proverbs said, "Even in laughter the heart may ache" (Proverbs 14:13). Peter spoke to believers who were both rejoicing and grieved at the same time (1 Peter 1:6). Jesus proclaimed, "Blessed are those who mourn" (Matthew 5:4) and then, just verses later, told persecuted believers to "rejoice and be glad" (v 12). And while Christ endured the cross "for the joy that was set before him" (Hebrews 12:2), we can't forget that his prayers rang out with "loud cries and tears" (5:7). Sorrow and joy may seem like contradicting emotions, but the Bible carries them together.

Paul encapsulated all of these examples when he said that he and his companions were "sorrowful, yet always rejoicing" (2 Corinthians 6:10). This is the paradox of faith: we are marked by both sadness and joy. Like an eclipse, we acknowledge the darkness and the light at the same time. Suffering hurts, sin dismantles, tragedies continue—and Jesus reigns, grace abounds, redemption will win. The authors of *Untangling Emotions* address this reality as they point out, "Life in this world means the delightful glories of God's handiwork always get the muck of sin and suffering on them." So how do believers respond? They continue: "We have no godly choice but to both mourn *and* rejoice."[27]

Becoming Eli's father enveloped me in this tension of *and*. His death emptied my soul *and* his brief life filled my heart; watching my wife suffer devastated me *and* her fierce motherly love captivated me; we felt incredibly lonely *and* unbelievably cared for by others; I thanked God for giving us Eli *and* wrestled with why he would take him away; the Lord confused me *and* the gospel comforted me. It often felt as if I needed to choose between the two, but God's word freed me up to try to hold both at the same time.

When you suffer, you might face pressure to choose between joy and sorrow. You may feel obligated towards joy because it seems like the faithful option. Or you might avoid rejoicing because you don't want to dismiss the pain you feel. But the Bible does not force you to decide between the two. To grow in faith, it seems, is to increase in our capacity to hold sorrow and joy simultaneously. You can groan *and* rejoice. So don't ignore the darkness. And don't forget the light.

Embracing this tension is not only key to walking through your own circumstances but also to navigating life alongside others. In Romans, Paul shows that sorrowful joy should permeate the entire Christian community. He tells believers: "Rejoice with those who rejoice, weep with those who weep" (Romans 12:15). The church is meant to be hospitable to both heartache and happiness.

We'll turn our attention to lament and community in the following chapters. But for now, we see that the body as a whole is to make space for joy and sorrow. The seasons you go through will often be different than those around you are experiencing. For you, it may be "a time to dance," while someone you know is experiencing "a time to mourn" (Ecclesiastes 3:4). But just like we hold joy and sorrow together as individuals, we're also meant to embrace this tension in our relationships. Sorrowful joy enables you to enter into others' mourning and celebration. You can join in others' happiness even when sadness grips your soul. And you can weep with others even when rejoicing marks your days.

JOY CAN COME *THROUGH* SORROW

Joy and sorrow can coexist, but there's another way they relate to each other. Sorrow can *produce* joy. To say that engaging sadness can cause rejoicing may sound unimaginable. You might think that wading in the depths of distress will only pull you further down. But Scripture shows that just the opposite can be true. Lament paves the path for rejoicing to occur.

Several passages showcase this movement. David encourages his readers, "Weeping may tarry for the night, but joy comes with the morning" (Psalm 30:5). Another psalmist offers the same hope: "Those who sow in tears shall reap with shouts of joy" (126:5). And Jesus told his disciples: "You will be sorrowful, but your sorrow will turn into joy" (John 16:20). Scripture holds out this promise that aching hearts can rejoice again.

One of the most powerful demonstrations of this is in the life of a man named Habakkuk. If you haven't spent much time with this prophet in your Bible, you'll want to get to know him. His resilient hope is worth our attention.

Calamity surrounds Habakkuk as he witnesses pervasive corruption amongst God's people, Israel. Instead of extending mercy, justice, and love, they are oppressive, violent, and cruel. And the Lord seems unmoved by their increasing injustice. Whereas Job struggled with God over personal tragedy, Habakkuk mourns the societal collapse around him. His story begins with a cry of complaint:

> O LORD, how long shall I cry for help,
>   and you will not hear?
> Or cry to you "Violence!"
>   and you will not save?
> Why do you make me see iniquity,
>   and why do you idly look at wrong?
> Destruction and violence are before me;
>   strife and contention arise. (Habakkuk 1:2-3)

Habakkuk explains his pain and expresses his protest. His questions of "How long?" and "Why?" reveal that his desperate cries have been ongoing and unanswered.

This time, God finally responds. But the Lord's answer stirs up even greater resistance from Habakkuk. The Lord reveals that he is about to use Israel's *enemy* to judge the injustice of God's people (v 5-11).

But to Habakkuk's mind, this is no solution. You and I would likely have similar concerns. Why would you punish injustice with worse injustice?

So Habakkuk protests again, this time with even stronger language (v 12-17). It's almost as if he feels that God misspoke the first time around. So he resolves to wait for a different answer from the Lord, concluding:

I will take my stand at my watchpost
  and station myself on the tower,
and look out to see what he will say to me,
  and what I will answer concerning my complaint.
                                        (Habakkuk 2:1)

The Lord's plan unsettles Habakkuk. His world is caving in. Tragedy has taken hold of his soul. The situation is about to get worse than he could have imagined. Will his heart ever sing again? And how will God react to such resistance?

Just as we've seen him do again and again, God responds to his perplexed prophet with patience (2:2-20). The Lord is not indifferent to the oppression that grieved Habakkuk. Nor is God upset with his servant's wrestling. Rather, as the commentator O. Palmer Robertson says, the Lord is "fully in sympathy with the prophet's agony."[28] And God promises to judge the unjust and sustain the faithful.

This honest conversation with God leads Habakkuk to a surprising transformation. While the imminent destruction makes his body and heart tremble (3:16), it does not silence his soul. Listen to Habakkuk's change of tone at the end of the book:

Though the fig tree should not blossom,
  nor fruit be on the vines,
the produce of the olive fail
  and the fields yield no food,
the flock be cut off from the fold
  and there be no herd in the stalls,

> *yet I will rejoice in the* LORD;
> *I will take joy in the God of my salvation.*
>
> *(Habakkuk 3:17-18)*

Habakkuk does not ignore the despair about to occur. Barren trees, withering plants, desolate farms—the storm clouds are getting darker. Yet he anchors himself in God's promises and clings to joy in the Lord. And he doesn't merely say these things, he *sings* them. The third and final chapter of the book is a worship song, composed for "the choirmaster: with stringed instruments" (v 19). In the midst of suffering, Habakkuk rejoices in the Lord.

So how did he get there? Habakkuk took two pivotal steps that, if we follow, can help us move from sorrow to rejoicing.

First, he *wrestled with the Lord.* When we hear the call to "rejoice in our sufferings" (Romans 5:3), most of us probably imagine something like Habakkuk's song in chapter 3: confident faith in the face of calamity. But we can't forget the beginning of his story. Before he could get there, Habakkuk needed to wrestle with God. He brought his questions and complaints into a conversation with the Lord. This allowed him to voice his struggles and then listen to God's response. His pain and protest in the beginning of the book produced petition and praise by the end. Lament enabled him to rejoice in suffering.

Habakkuk joins a chorus of other believers whose sorrow turned to joy, whose lament produced rejoicing. Scenes in the lives of Abraham, David, and Jesus all show us a similar movement. Wrestling can lead to rejoicing.

This is not to say that rejoicing in suffering can *only* happen if lament occurs first. There are plenty of biblical examples where trust is almost instinctual for believers. For instance, Psalm 23 shows David's quiet confidence in the Lord: "Even though I walk through the valley of the shadow of death, I will fear no evil" (v 4). God can give his people surprising composure in suffering. But it's important to recognize lament as an authorized and frequent path towards rejoicing in trials. After all, David may have written Psalm 23, but more than half of the psalms he penned were laments.

The rejoicing that resounds in the midst of suffering does not sidestep sorrow—it rises through it. The Lord meets you in your lament and gently brings you toward deeper joy. You wrestle with a patient God who can restore your soul. It often takes time. Days, weeks, years. But you can wrestle, assured that sorrow will not have the final word.

Habakkuk's second step was to *remember God's redemption*. The situation in Israel offered little to celebrate, so Habakkuk rooted himself in something beyond his circumstances. What ultimately stirred his heart to rejoice? The storyline of the Lord's rescue. Habakkuk's song wove together a tapestry of images to retell stories of God's power and gracious salvation from across the Old Testament (Habakkuk 3:3-15). He recalled images of God creating the universe, rescuing his people in the exodus, bringing them through the wilderness, and delivering them into the promised land. Past rescue assured Habakkuk of future redemption, which enabled present rejoicing. This didn't change Habakkuk's situation, nor did it erase his pain. But it tethered him to hope that would sustain him in his suffering.

We, too, have a redemption story to recite—God's rescue culminated in the cross of Jesus. When Paul helped mourning Christians grieve with hope, he encouraged them to do the same thing Habakkuk did. Look *back* to Jesus' death and resurrection and look *forward* to Christ's return (1 Thessalonians 4:13-18). Past rescue, future redemption, present rejoicing.

It's tempting to grasp at fragile hopes when trials come. For example, after we lost Eli, some tried to console us with the fact that we were young—we still had time to have more children. And there was a part of me that wanted to cling to that. But more children weren't guaranteed. More children would not bring Eli back. More children wouldn't prevent more suffering. More children would not satisfy our souls. Eventually, we did plead with the Lord to expand our family. But Habakkuk's faith challenged us and shaped our prayers. Our longing could only resolve in Jesus. His death, resurrection, and return are the only true anchor for aching hearts.

Suffering can disorient you. It can cause you to wrestle with God like never before, to ask questions you've never considered, to feel pain you never thought possible. But as darkness descends, don't forget the light of the gospel.

Remember the cross. It is irrefutable proof that God loves you and knows your pain. Jesus' scars proclaim that he has done something about sin and suffering, and he will finish what he started.

Remember the resurrection. The empty tomb is your receipt of redemption. Jesus left death in the grave, declaring that nothing you face will triumph over you in the end. Your sorrow will not have the final say.

And remember that Christ will return. Your soul may ache until your last breath. But the day is coming when the Lord will wipe away your tears and pain forever.

Take joy in the God of your salvation.

In the days following the initial diagnosis, the anticipation of Eli's eventual death made lifting my voice feel impossible. I couldn't believe that my heart could sing again. But as my sorrow began to mingle with joy during the pregnancy, and my wrestling urged me to cling to the gospel, I realized: I can still sing to Eli. I would have the rest of my life to grieve the songless nights without him, but the remaining days with my son would no longer be silent.

So I went out, bought a ukulele, and we started the bedtime routine I had dreamed about. For the remainder of the pregnancy, we ended the day with singing. I would nuzzle up to Jillian's belly so that Eli could hear my voice and I would fight through tears to sing to my son. Some of them were classic hits that Jillian and I loved. Other songs were entertaining, providing some laughter for a change. But the hardest to sing were the hymns and worship songs embedded with promises that we needed to hear. Singing to our son enabled us to rejoice in suffering.

The song that rose to the top of the list was a hymn we sang at our wedding, "This is My Father's World." Its final verse rings out much like Habakkuk's. It acknowledges the darkness, recognizes the light, and remembers the gospel. Not only did it become part of this bedtime rhythm, it became an anthem of hope for our family. We sang it at night when Eli was with us. We sang it as we held him one last time before leaving the hospital. We sang it with family and friends at his memorial service. And we sing it every year on his birthday while sitting at his grave:

> *This is my Father's world,*
> *O let me ne'er forget*
> *That though the wrong*
> *Seems oft so strong*
> *God is the ruler yet.*
> *This is my Father's world,*
> *The battle is not done:*
> *Jesus who died*
> *Will be satisfied*
> *And earth and heav'n be one.*

The sorrow you face is real. The wrong you feel is strong. But they will not have the final say. You can take joy in the God of your salvation. Jesus died, rose, and will one day resolve all that unsettles your soul. Your heart will sing again.

BEING HONEST WITH EACH OTHER

PART 2

CHAPTER 6

WEEP TOGETHER

Jillian and I hid behind our pastor as he rushed us out of the sanctuary. His broad frame shielded us from onlookers, who became blurry figures as we sped past them with tear-filled eyes. It was our weeping during worship that prompted this rescue. Eli's death was parading around our souls. As we turned to God in our pain, grief dismantled us in the pew. So our pastor brought us to another room where we could cry freely. He climbed down into our darkness to listen, weep with us, and pray.

At the time, this escape was helpful. But looking back now, it concerns me. It felt appropriate and necessary to be ushered out of church to weep—but it shouldn't have. Sorrow should not have to be escorted out of the sanctuary.

This is no critique of our pastor. No, he was loving us well. He instinctively knew we needed to release our grief.

His impulse was right—that's exactly what our hearts required. We needed to weep and wrestle with the Lord.

The problem is that this is meant to be a *part of* corporate worship, not *apart from* it. But many churches in Western culture gravitate towards positive emotions and the celebratory parts of Scripture. Still others tend more toward emotional reserve, where any big expression of feeling would be out of place, especially displays of sadness and grief. We leave little room for lament in our songs and prayers. So our pastor, a good shepherd, created space for our sorrow elsewhere. In another room. In private.

I am deeply grateful for his tangible compassion. We were hurting. We were seen. We were helped. But many carry sorrow that goes unreleased, unnoticed, and unaddressed. It's unfortunately common to hear that church is one of the hardest places to be in the midst of hardship.

Maybe you have limped into church, weighed down by things like sadness, fear, or disappointment. Yet the place you hoped to find healing and refuge left you feeling hurt and alone. As the body of Christ joined together in praise, you felt dislocated in your pain.

This is not how it's supposed to be. The church is meant to be a place of sorrowful joy, where we not only "rejoice with those who rejoice," but also "weep with those who weep" (Romans 12:15). In this chapter, we're going to turn our attention to lament at the communal level. Faithful groaning is not only meant for private conversations with the Lord. The Bible urges us to seize hope through honest worship, *together*. Sorrow belongs in the sanctuary.

KNOWING OUR HYMNBOOK

Sorrow's place in church is evidenced in the Psalms. These cherished poems are not just meant to instruct our personal time with God. While they certainly deepen our individual relationships with the Lord, their initial use was communal. More than that, they were *songs* for gathered believers. They "were intended to be presented—performed, if you will—within community worship."[29] Most psalms include descriptions with information like song titles, composer names, musical terms, and liturgical cues. If you want to know how our ancestors worshiped, listen to the Psalms. This is the hymnbook of God's people.[30]

And the Psalms are still meant to shape our worship today. Paul commands believers to sing "psalms and hymns and spiritual songs" when they gather (Colossians 3:16; Ephesians 5:19). Commenting on these verses, Christopher Ash says that "while we cannot conclude that the early church used *only* Old Testament Psalms, these formed a significant, and perhaps the main, part of their Spirit-inspired singing."[31] But listen closely to the psalmists' songs and you will hear something strikingly different from ours: their corporate worship expressed an overwhelming amount of struggle.

Weeping and wrestling take up much of this songbook's playlist. In fact, the largest category of psalms is songs of lament—accounting for over a third of the book (see Appendix A). We've seen this in previous chapters, but it bears repeating again: *One out of every three* songs in the Psalms is a hymn of heartache. God's people sang often about pain, confusion, and trouble.

This may surprise you, since the goal of worshiping God is, as one modern songwriter and worship leader has put it, to "magnify his greatness."[32] Cries and complaints don't seem appropriate for Sunday morning. It may be one thing to wrestle privately with God, but it hardly feels holy to sing publicly about despair and difficult questions. Yet the Bible puts songs of anguish alongside songs of adulation. Both are to be brought to God because both bring him glory. The fact that the title of the book, Psalms, means "Praises," teaches us that "the whole range of the psalms—from adoration and thanks to the needy cry for help (even the desolate moan of Psalm 88)—praises God when offered to him in the gathered worship of his people."[33] In other words, lament is not something we do *before* we can worship. Lament *is* worship.

Songs of sorrow are to be a fundamental part of how we approach the Lord together. As Mark Vroegop says, "Too many people think real worship only means an upbeat and happy demeanor. But grief-filled prayers of pain while seeking God are among the deepest expressions of worship."[34] Groaning together glorifies the Lord.

Lament's frequency in Scripture means that our songs and prayers do not need to sugarcoat life in the wilderness. Rather, our worship should deal honestly with the ravages of sin and suffering. The tone and content of what we do when we gather should make space for experiences like loneliness, anxiety, depression, doubt, injustice, grief, sickness, and abuse—all of which are expressed in the Psalms.

God's hymnbook is a compilation of sorrowful joy. It resounds with celebration *and* sadness, confidence *and* questions, gratitude *and* grief, trust *and* tragedy—all honoring the Lord in the gathering of God's people. Scripture prescribes an expression of worship wide enough to include the depths of despair, the heights of happiness, and every hill and valley in between.

NEGLECTING OUR HERITAGE

But a close look reveals that our worship today tends to stay on the mountain top.

Several surveys show that lament has been fading from worship for generations. A comparison between mainline hymnals and the Psalms led the researcher Glenn Pemberton to conclude that "we have almost completely lost the biblical language of lament ... it has become a curious museum piece in our Bibles. Expressions of unresolved pain, confusion, desperation, and sorrow—in other words, lament—are nearly extinct."[35]

Professor of Biblical Theology Denise Hopkins also examined the use of lament in major denominations and found that "laments are noticeably absent as hymns."[36]

She notes that if we do use a lament from the Bible as a basis for a hymn, it's common that "the guts of lament are cut out."[37] In other words, we tend to use the positive portions of Scripture for our songs but leave behind the honest struggle and emotional intensity.[38] Her study also revealed the concerning trend that several hymns "discourage any expression of doubt and questions."[39] So not only do our hymns omit biblical lament, some also explicitly oppose God's invitation to wrestle with him.

The pattern continues with new songs. Study the top charts of worship music and you will be struck by the absence of psalm-like wrestling. Positive proclamations and confident celebrations dominate our lyrics. The exceptions—the two things we do lament—are our own sinfulness and Jesus' suffering. Of course, both of these merit our sorrow. But sufferers can be left thinking that they either need to repent of their sin or rejoice that their suffering will never be as bad as Jesus'. As Tim Keller observes:

> There is seldom a place provided for lamentation in the church ... many do not give sufferers the freedom to weep and cry out, "Where are you Lord? Why are you not helping me?" [40]

So what, specifically, is present in the Psalms yet missing in our worship? Consider the four rhythms of lament in comparison to the songs that you sing on Sunday.

Pain is rarely explained in our lyrics. When sorrow is included, it's often just a brief mention before proclaiming

God's deliverance. We tend to sing about suffering in passing and in the past tense. Unlike the Psalms, our lyrics rarely include struggles we might be feeling and experiencing *now*. Worship, then, puts pain in the rearview mirror, even though sorrow is a present reality for many in the pews.

Protests are virtually non-existent as well. Instead of an honest struggle with God, most songs about suffering express our need to simply trust him in the storm. We don't cry out "why?" or "how long?" like believers in the Bible do. Whereas the Lord expects and encourages relational tension, our songs rarely allow us to wrestle with God.

It's surprising to find that even *petitions* are rare in our lyrics. For some reason, asking the Lord to do things like listen, rescue, and deliver are no longer common. Our songs may *declare* our dependence on the Lord, but psalmists *demonstrate* their reliance through desperate requests.

And *praise* is not an *eventual* reality fought for through pain, protest, and petition. Praise stands alone as the constant refrain. This ironically results in worship that's monotone. Different chords, tempos, volume, instruments, and lyrics may create the impression of variety. But the vast majority of songs belong to the same category of sorrowless praise.

So instead of making space for sorrow as Scripture does, our songs are saturated in joy, confidence, and awe. We humble our hearts before God, adore him for his attributes and actions, ponder his promises, confess our sins, glorify his goodness, declare our dependence, and confirm our commitment. To be sure, these are all profoundly biblical and God-honoring. It's right that we do these things. I'm not proposing that we throw away our praise songs altogether—only that we add what is lacking. In his book on corporate worship, hymn-writer Matt Merker helpfully summarizes our worship with three categories: *gravity, gratitude,* and *gladness.*[41] But Scripture would add a fourth category that we often neglect—*groaning.*

When we omit the groaning of lament in corporate worship—not just in our singing, but also in our prayers and liturgy—we forsake a foundational rhythm that God established for his people. As Old Testament scholar Walter Brueggemann stresses, "a church that goes on singing 'happy songs' in the face of raw reality is doing something very different from what the Bible itself does."[42] And neglecting our biblical heritage significantly impacts individuals and communities.

WORSHIPING WITH HONESTY

It's important to note that lament's omission has not been intentionally devised by any individual or group. It's not as though believers attend church with the aim of excluding others' sorrow. Nor do I suggest that songwriters have purposefully ignored sufferers. And I certainly don't want to give the impression that all our pastors and worship leaders are guiding us into false or ungenuine faith. But we can't ignore the reality that Bible-informed wrestling is often left out of our worship gatherings. And we struggle to shape our services in a way that provides space for the kind of honesty we see in Scripture.

If we acknowledge this, and understand the power and purpose of corporate groaning, we can take steps to recover our heritage of honest worship. So what would church feel like if we embraced communal lament?

Sufferers would feel welcomed. When worship is primarily positive, those who are struggling can experience further isolation. They're often given three options in worship: sing through the pain, stand silent through the praise, or stay away from church altogether until their hurt subsides. Theologian Carl Trueman explains what this suppression of sorrow does:

> By excluding the cries of loneliness, dispossession, and desolation from its worship, the church has effectively silenced and excluded the voices of those who are themselves lonely, dispossessed, and desolate, both inside and outside the church.[43]

But lament transforms worship into a profound act of hospitality. Instead of relegating misery to the margins, despair can have a voice alongside the celebration. Singing songs of sorrow invites strugglers to bring their troubles and difficult questions. Including pain and protest in prayer affirms that it's okay to wrestle with God. The Lord does not expect us to pretend our difficulties have dissolved because it's Sunday. He invites weary souls to worship honestly. Lament welcomes sufferers and gives them a song to sing.

Imagine the impact, not just on burdened believers, but also for outsiders curious to know what God is like. Lament puts on display an empathetic and gracious God who hears our cries, welcomes our honesty, and groans alongside us. And it points to a weeping Savior, acquainted with grief, who took our sorrows and sin to suffer in our place. Lament preaches the gospel.

The body would be unified. We can sometimes treat corporate worship as a gathering of people having individual experiences with the Lord. And while it's an important time to engage the Lord personally, we're also meant to edify others' faith (Hebrews 10:24-25). In fact, in the same passages where Paul encourages psalm-shaped worship, he also tells believers to sing and address *one another* (Colossians 3:16; Ephesians 5:19). As we worship alongside others, we don't just stand *with* them. We sing *to* them. We pray *for* them. Our eyes are not only meant to look forward and upward on Sundays—we're supposed to look around. The circumstances of those around us are meant to be on our hearts as we worship.

But floods of confident praise can drown out our ability to empathize with brothers and sisters who are struggling. Communal lament, however, brings their pain to our attention. It reminds those who aren't suffering about those who are. They can cry out on behalf of those in the pews, in their community, and around the world. In worship we can display the unity of God's people: "If one member suffers, all suffer together; if one member is honored, all rejoice together" (1 Corinthians 12:26). Praise connects us with those who celebrate; lament binds us to others' burdens.

Believers would be equipped. What we do in corporate worship helps to mold us as Christ-followers. Music has a special way of getting under our skin. You probably can't recite your pastor's most recent sermon word for word, but you can doubtless recall countless songs by memory. Similarly, our habits shape us. Our repeated practices forge who we are and what we believe. In other words, worship is not just an activity you participate in, it's a practice that changes you. So when our songs hammer on optimism and confidence, while avoiding the God-ordained process of lament, they train us to do the same. Not only can this dilute our expectations that trials will come—it can also deprive us of the language God gave us to process and endure suffering.

This may help to explain why so many are surprised to hear that lament is biblically appropriate. Our positive worship has shaped us to believe that immediate praise and quiet confidence are the only faith-filled responses to suffering. And I can't help but wonder if this is a significant reason why we struggle with difficult emotions—both ours and others'. I find it no coincidence that the platitudes and advice that circulate around calamity carry the same positive tone and sentiment of our worship songs.

But lament can reshape the discomfort that we feel toward sorrow. If lament becomes a common practice together, it will become a familiar part of faith for individuals. We won't shy away from sad realities, unsettling prayers, or difficult questions. This will allow believers to navigate their own difficulties with honesty and hope. And, as we'll see more in the following chapters, it will enable us to walk alongside others with patience and compassion.

RECOVERING OUR HERITAGE

If lament takes up a third of the Psalms, it ought to be a regular part of our worship as well. This doesn't mandate a particular ratio of lament to praise. But it seems that lament should be frequent and familiar when we gather. Every week, there are trials to grieve in our lives, communities, nation, and world. Lament gives us the powerful opportunity to confront and endure suffering together with honest hope.

Admittedly, this would require the landscape of corporate worship to shift. We need songwriters to compose more hymns of heartache, leaders to model lament in prayer, and services to allow space for sorrow. And if God has given you any of those roles, please use your gifts and platform to help the church recover God's gift of lament. But even if you're not involved in shaping your worship gatherings, you can be a catalyst for change in your community. Here are two simple ways to take a step in that direction.

First, make lament common in personal worship. When you pray on your own, include the four aspects of lament. Use the Psalms as a springboard for your honest prayers. It will likely take time before it becomes comfortable, especially adding pain and protest into prayers. But it will deepen your engagement with the Lord in response to suffering. Similarly, you could listen to lament songs regularly. Good options to start with are "Lament" by Seacoast Worship, "Wake Up Jesus" by The Porter's Gate, or "Lord From Sorrows Deep I Call" by Matt Boswell and Matt Papa. (For more suggestions, see Appendix B.) Cultivate a habit of lamenting through prayer and song—and recognize the groaning as worship.

Second, make space for shared sorrow. When you gather with other believers, help create an environment where honesty is welcome. Assume what the Bible assumes: suffering is often present wherever people gather. So think of others as you worship—how might the service feel for someone who is hurting? If you know someone there who is suffering, let them know you were thinking of them during the service. A confident prayer may have been hard for them to agree with, praise may have felt impossible to sing, or a lament may have given voice to their sorrow. And don't feel ashamed if you're the one struggling to sing. Seek to make space for sorrow in your conversations, too (which we'll discuss more in the next two chapters). In the questions you ask, the way you steer conversations, and the way you respond to people's difficulties—speak in a way that models and invites honesty. Where there are opportunities to pray with others, don't be afraid to cry out like people do in the Bible.

And while you may not have direct involvement in leading your worship service, you could speak to the people who do. Reach out to your leaders and start conversations about bringing lament into the service. Ask your pastor or worship team their thoughts on lament and its prevalence in Scripture. Share with them the burden you have for sufferers and the hope that can be found through honest worship.

I've seen several communities experience the power of lament simply because one or two people humbly cultivated it and advocated for it. You can be the one to pave the way for your community's recovery of lament.

At Eli's memorial service, our sorrow was not only welcomed, it was shared. We used Psalm 44 in a call-and-response reading for the congregation. Up until that point, many individuals had shown us compassion through various notes, gestures, and gifts. But in this moment, hundreds of voices cried in unison with us. We called out together:

> *Awake! Why are you sleeping, O Lord?*
>   *Rouse yourself! Do not reject us forever!*
> *Why do you hide your face?*
>   *Why do you forget our affliction and oppression?*
> *For our soul is bowed down to the dust;*
>   *our belly clings to the ground.*

Rise up; come to our help!
  Redeem us for the sake of your steadfast love!
                                    (Psalm 44:23-26)

Our grief was not ours alone to bear. Through lament, our friends and family took hold of our heartache. They made our sorrows their own. Our questions became their questions. Our groans became their groans. Their cries on our behalf resounded: we were not alone.

This is the power of communal lament. It welcomes those who are weeping and allows others to wrestle on their behalf. May each of our churches be a community that offers lasting hope, found through honest worship. Sorrow belongs in the sanctuary.

CHAPTER 7

LET OTHERS IN

"How are you?" I didn't know what to say. My acquaintance's simple question felt impossible to answer. Eli had just died and the edges of my grief were sharp. But an honest response to the question wasn't actually expected. And unloading my sorrow on someone I barely knew wouldn't have been helpful for either of us. We were just saying hi in passing, exchanging polite pleasantries and moving on with our day. Yet the question still provoked my soul. How was I?

Barely breathing. Not sleeping. Wrestling with God. I miss my son. Life has no color. Sorrow has no end. Anxious, angry, and afraid. Battling bitterness. I'm a childless father. A heartbroken husband. I'm terrified. Hopeless. Numb.

I bypassed the real answers and opted for the proper formula. "Good, you?"

Shallow, daily transactions like this had occurred prior to Eli without any agitation. Now, they felt like an assault. These short conversations unleashed my grief while requiring that I keep it under control. They gave the illusion that most people were doing "good," and those of us who weren't should at least pretend that we were. I knew this wasn't true—burdens of various kinds weigh most people down. But when everyone's expected to *say* they're good, it can feel inappropriate to admit that you're not.

Now, I don't intend to rewrite the etiquette of everyday interactions. And I don't advocate that we all start baring our souls to strangers. But it raises a question worth considering. How should we speak about our difficulties with others? We've covered a lot about how to weep and wrestle with the Lord. So far most of our discussion has concerned the vertical, between us and God. But we now turn to the horizontal aspect of lament and how to talk with others about our trials.

When you're struggling, how do you tend to speak about it? Some feel the pressure to tell their stories with confidence. So they either rush towards positivity or wait until they're past their pain to speak about it. Others don't hesitate to openly share their raw emotion, whether in person or online. And some don't feel the need to talk about their struggles at all.

Biblical lament cuts through each of these options and offers a different way. It shows us the value of speaking honestly about what ails us, while doing so with wisdom and intention. The key is to recognize the purpose behind our sharing—you can speak about your difficulties in a way that invites help or offers support. Others can help you lament. And your laments can help others.

OTHERS CAN HELP YOU LAMENT

It can be hard to admit our need for help. We want to be competent, resilient, and strong. We prefer to be known as depend*able*, not depend*ent*. Relying on others can make us feel weak. Dependence feels like it goes against every fiber in us—yet it's built into the fabric of our existence. The Lord created us to lean on each other.

Think of Moses, who tried to shepherd God's people alone. His father-in-law saw the dangers of solitary leadership and told him, "What you are doing is not good ... the thing is too heavy for you" (Exodus 18:17-18). So Moses learned the gift of delegation and teamwork (v 24-26). Or consider Queen Esther, who relied on her uncle Mordecai's guidance as she ascended and acclimated to the throne (Esther 2:5-23). Paul, too, leaned on others for prayer (1 Thessalonians 5:25), encouragement (2 Timothy 1:16), practical needs (Philippians 4:14-18), and support in ministry (2 Timothy 4:11). Even Jesus and his disciples depended on a faithful band of women "who provided for them out of their means" (Luke 8:3).

These all echo the first "not good" of the Bible, which occurred before sin invaded: "It is not good that the man should be alone" (Genesis 2:18). God created us to rely not just on him, but on others for help. And he saved us to be part of a community—the church. We stand together under the same banner as Moses: "You are not able to do it alone" (Exodus 18:18).

Our everyday dependence becomes all the more necessary when heartache comes. Suffering can cause us to distance ourselves from people, but it's crucial to bring others into our sorrows. We need support as we wrestle with the Lord and endure the trials of life. So how can we look to others for help as we lament?

Jesus offers us an example of how to do this well. We've already heard his lamenting in Gethsemane. Look again at how he relied on his friends before wrestling with the Father.

> Then Jesus went with them to a place called Gethsemane, and he said to his disciples, "Sit here, while I go over there and pray." And taking with him Peter and the two sons of Zebedee, he began to be sorrowful and troubled. Then he said to them, "My soul is very sorrowful, even to death; remain here, and watch with me." And going a little farther he fell on his face and prayed. (Matthew 26:36-39)

It's remarkable to consider that Jesus, who "upholds the universe by the word of his power" (Hebrews 1:3), leaned on other people. Many had cried out to him for help, but now he asked others for support. Jesus shows us three important dimensions of relying on others as we lament.

He relied on a few. Earlier that week, Jesus had entered Jerusalem surrounded by enthusiastic crowds. His ministry to multitudes over the years had earned him influencer status. The city, already full of commotion because of the Passover, stirred at his arrival. But the noise of Jesus' triumphal entry faded quickly. The place that welcomed him with excitement would host his execution. And as Jesus anticipated his crucifixion, he didn't turn to the crowds for support. He gathered just his dearest friends.

Only his disciples shared the privilege of joining him in Gethsemane. But did you notice that he was even more selective than that? He brought Peter and the two sons of Zebedee, James and John, further along with him before he prayed. This inner circle had enjoyed special access on other occasions.[44] But those were miraculous and exhilarating events. Now they joined Jesus in a moment of anguish. Peter, James, and John were invited to witness their Savior's agony and his wrestling with the Father. Jesus entrusted his deepest despair to his closest companions.

He included them in the process. Jesus shared his unresolved pain with his disciples *before* he prayed. He knew he needed to plead with the Father. But he didn't wait until afterwards to talk about it. He felt no need to pretend like he was further along in his wrestling, no pressure to put a positive spin on his sadness. The praise would come eventually, but not yet. Jesus displays the value of bringing others into the process as we work through our laments with God.

He understood their limits. Jesus relied on his friends, but with realistic expectations. He understood that their help could only go so far. Prior to this scene, he told them that they would abandon him later that night (Matthew 26:30-35). And soon after he began praying, they couldn't stay awake (v 40-46). Yet Jesus still invited them into his grief. He shows us that the support others offer us is necessary, but limited. They can listen. They can help us process. They can offer presence, comfort, and practical help. But they aren't perfect. They won't get everything right, even with the best intentions. And they can't fix our pain. God is the one we need to struggle with and ultimately rely on. This is why the greatest companion is someone who points you to the Lord and helps you wrestle with him.

When Jillian and I first found out Eli's diagnosis, we realized how incapable we were of navigating the shadows alone. But talking to others initially felt impossible. The uniqueness of Eli's condition, along with the distinct sting of anticipated child loss, made it seem like no one would understand. We quickly learned, however, that compassion would not keep its distance. Our closest friends and family asked, "How are you?" and wanted to hear the honest answer. They helped us process our raw emotions and visceral struggles, gently turning us to lament before the Lord. Their help had limitations: they couldn't save Eli, answer all our questions, or heal our hearts. But they pleaded with God on our behalf, listened to our cries, and tended to our sorrows. And they're still with us to this day.

As you lament, look to others for help. Bring a few others into the process as you work through your difficulties. This is not an easy task. Trusting others can be risky, finding companions can be difficult, and sharing vulnerably can be unnerving. But you were not meant to bear your burdens alone.

YOUR LAMENTS CAN HELP OTHERS

That's exactly how I feel. I thought this as I grieved Eli's death, not on one occasion, but on too many to count, as I read the experiences of others. The journal C.S. Lewis kept after his wife died put words to my sorrow, like when he refers to loss as an amputation—an absence you may learn to live with, but an emptiness you will never forget.[45] The laments of Nicholas Wolterstorff, another grieving father, helped me stumble through death's shadow. Like when he acknowledged how grief stole his desire to grasp for joy: "Instead of rowing, I float."[46] I found many companions in my pain. Their wrestling made me feel less alone, their laments gave me language to groan with, and their faith helped me ache in hope.

Personal laments, I have found, don't just get *us* through the storm. They can also sustain others in their suffering.

The most prevalent example of this in Scripture occurs through the life of David. He encountered all kinds of trials and tragedies. He faced the ravages of war and endured great burdens as a king. Enemies persecuted him. Corrupt leaders pursued him. Allies abandoned him. He lost companions and grieved the loss of children. Those he led doubted his authority. Those he loved betrayed his confidence. He suffered sickness and sleeplessness, anxiety and loneliness, fear and despair. So how did David, Israel's most prominent king, share his sorrow with others?

He wrote songs. You might not expect such a mighty warrior to make melody with his voice. But this fierce soldier, decorated general, and powerful ruler was also "the sweet psalmist of Israel." (2 Samuel 23:1). He composed about half of the psalms, and the majority of the ones he wrote were laments. Not only did he acknowledge his dependence, he shared it with others. He made his personal wrestling public.

David's songs have helped innumerable sufferers over thousands of years, and continue to do so to this day. They carry such value that Jesus used them at his hour of greatest need. His final words on the cross twisted together multiple threads of David's laments.

Jesus groaned, "I thirst" (John 19:28), using the explained pain from Psalm 69. He cried out, "My God, my God, why have you forsaken me?" (Mark 15:34), a protest first penned in Psalm 22. And Jesus quoted Psalm 31 in his final submission: "Father, into your hands I commit my spirit!" (Luke 23:46). Jesus took up David's laments as his own. One suffering king gave voice to another.

True, Jesus fulfilled Scripture in a way that was utterly unique—under the Holy Spirit's inspiration, the psalms were always intended as portraits of Christ.

But there's something else that each of us can take from David's example. The lesson is not that we all ought to become songwriters in our sorrow. Nor does it require that you publicize your pain. And it certainly doesn't mean that you have to share your story before you're ready. Rather, it shows that God can use your laments to help someone else. We won't pen Scripture the way that David did; but as Spirit-filled believers, God can nonetheless use our words to minister to others.

So where do we begin? David shows us how lament can shape the way you talk about your trials. We can share with honesty, wisdom, and hope.

Share honestly. David wrote many laments in the midst of the storm, *before* rescue came.[47] Other times, he told a before-and-after story through his song—but even those often contain present-tense wrestling.[48] His laments often maintain the language of how it *feels*, not how it *felt*. He included his questions and complaints as he experienced them. Why is that important? Suffering's intensity often subsides as time goes on, which can lead to diluting the way someone speaks about it. But David preserved the potency of his pain, even after God delivered him.

You don't have to wait until you're through your suffering to talk about it. And you don't need to soften the intensity of your experience. You can talk about your sorrows and questions before they've resolved. And it's alright if praise and joy are still anticipated realities.

Share your present and recurring troubles—it can help others put words to their sorrows. Remind them that they're not alone.

Share wisely. While Scripture encourages honesty, it also promotes discretion. David was direct—but he wasn't unbridled. He ensured that, however honest his complaints, they still honored the Lord. His prayers and songs have since been heard and repeated by countless believers—leading God's people on the trajectory of trust in their trials.

When sharing your story honestly in order to help others, be thoughtful about what you say and how you say it. *Truthful* does not mean *unfiltered*. For example, many things that I've shared with my wife, counselor, and closest friends would not be beneficial to include in a sermon or this book. And there are parts of my journal that will only remain between me and the Lord. It's not because I'm ashamed of what I said. But there were unprocessed emotions that I needed to work through before I could share them in a helpful way.

This is all the more reason to keep pressing into the Lord and bringing others in to help. Their support allows you to work through your difficulties. Ask them to help you share about your suffering. Merge honesty with wisdom as you tell your story to help others.

Share hopefully. All of David's laments were oriented toward the Lord. He directed his pain, protests, petitions, and praise to God—enabling others to do the same. His songs remind us that we have a heavenly Father who is listening, even when we struggle to believe he is. They point us to Jesus, the promised one, whose love culminated in his sacrificial death, who rescues and redeems. And Jesus' use of David's songs demonstrates that the Lord doesn't only *hear* our laments; in the person of Christ he also laments *with* us and *for* us.

Suffering has a way of loosening our grip on God's promises. But lament helps us cling to Christ and remind us that he has not let us go. Share your tear-soaked trust in the Lord and point people to hope that lasts.

You can follow David's example and let your story impact others. You can help the hurting by sharing your heartache and hope. For most of us, this will take place in daily interactions. We're all connected to other people who carry burdens of their own. You can help them by honestly, wisely, and hopefully sharing what you've gone through. Everyday conversations can have profound impact. Whether it's something you experienced a long time ago, or something you're going through now, God can use your story to affect others.

Some people reading this will have the opportunity to talk about their trials in the public sphere. If your suffering leads you to share something on social media, tell your testimony in a small group or church, start a blog, publish a book, compose a song, create art, write poetry, or establish an organization—let lament guide and shape what you say. Give voice to pain, protest, petition, and praise in what you share.

Whether it's through personal conversation or public opportunities, share with honesty, wisdom, and hope.

One of my first opportunities to share publicly about Eli was through a sermon I gave at our ministry's annual Fall Student Conference. Before preaching, I sat alone backstage, overcome with sorrow as the singing came to a close. My assigned text was Romans 8:31-39, which promises that trials will not triumph over those in Christ. I initially accepted the task with excitement, but this was before we knew we would lose our son. We found out about Eli's condition shortly after I agreed to preach. Now, I wrestled with finding hope in the very truths I was meant to proclaim.

Death's shadow engulfed my sermon preparation. We were still in the middle of the pregnancy that we knew would end in devastation. I considered backing out. But Scripture had already convinced me of what this passage declared: suffering does not negate God's promises. Believing this in the midst of comfort is utterly different than proclaiming it in the grip of grief. My conviction, however, had not changed. So I stumbled on stage, shared our story, and preached through tears and timid belief.

This was no act of courage. Like Paul, I spoke "in weakness and in fear and much trembling" (1 Corinthians 2:3). Afterwards, I staggered back to sit with my pregnant wife. My sermon, "More Than Conquerors," already felt untrue. This seemed nothing like victory. My own words agitated me. But God's word gently reminded me that even though my faith was weak, Christ would hold us fast.

It has been a battle to surrender to the Lord and the story he has written for our family. I would much rather have Eli in my arms than a sermon at a conference or my name on this book. But I am not the author of my life. Only by his grace, the gift of lament, and the help of others have I been able to say, "Not my will, but yours." And part of trusting God with our story has been sharing it with others. Despite the difficulty, it's an honor to declare my son's worth, my Savior's grace, and my honest struggle in the midst of our suffering. And as Eli's dad, I consider it a somber privilege if his life and death produce in others honest faith and hope in Christ.

Your laments can also help sustain sufferers. You can point them to a God who hears our cries, welcomes our wrestling, knows our pain, and restores our souls.

CHAPTER 8

BEAR THEIR BURDENS

Our funeral director sat at our dining room table. This stranger in our home had immediately become someone of indescribable significance. He had been entrusted with the sacred and exclusive duty of taking care of Eli's body and burial. We discussed details that no parent should have to plan: writing an obituary, choosing a casket, deciding on a gravestone. Arranging your child's funeral vandalizes your soul in a way that can't be forgotten. But as our hearts wavered between numbing disbelief and paralyzing pain, our funeral director repeated a phrase that was a balm in our anguish:

"It's what we do."

This was his tagline as he ran through everything he and his wife would do to relieve our burden as best they could. Not charging us for their services. *It's what we do.* Finding financial aid to pay for all additional costs. *"It's what we do."* Connecting us with a ministry that handmakes and donates children's caskets. *"It's what we do."* As a bereaved father and believer himself, our funeral director assured us that we would be taken care of and our son would be remembered.

His phrase has reverberated beyond our conversation that day. *"It's what we do"* does not just explain his empathetic generosity, it captures the thoughtfulness of so many others who have walked with us through death's shadow. We haven't been exempt from wounding words or hurtful avoidance. But countless cards, gifts, gestures, and tears have helped us endure. Each act of compassion could be tagged with the line, *"It's what we do."*

For seven chapters we have explored various aspects of faithful groaning. Lament has shown us how honest faith can produce enduring hope. In the last two chapters, we shifted from the vertical to the horizontal, seeing how lament impacts our relationships with one another. And we began to turn outward, considering how our stories can provide help to others. As this book comes to a close, I want to take a final step to show how God moves us from hurting, to heard, to helping. Lament is not just how we pray through *our* sorrows, it's also how we walk with others through theirs.

If you're suffering right now, please don't view this chapter as some sort of pressure to move along quicker in your sorrow. Feel free to skip this chapter until you're ready— something you can return to when you're in a position to help others. Or you could share it with the friends who are trying to walk alongside you in this season.

Those of us walking alongside others have the profound opportunity to love them like Christ. But walking with sufferers can be difficult. We fear saying something hurtful, dread the discomfort of silence, or struggle with how to respond. It's easier to offer quick platitudes instead of faithful presence: to deliver truth without tears rather than sit and weep. But lament gives us a powerful tool to come alongside those who are struggling. It allows us to reject shallow responses, find the courage to sit in silence, and escape the pressure to fix things or rush people towards healing. Lament helps us reflect our Savior's compassion as we listen and groan with the hurting. We weep with those who weep. It's what we do.

PRAY

One of the first ways we can help people is by praying for them. But we can easily overlook lament as a crucial way to intercede for others.

Throughout this book, we have talked about lament primarily as a way to pray through your own difficulties. But Scripture also shows that it's how we should pray for one another. David mourned the mistreatment of the poor, fatherless, and oppressed (Psalm 10), and lamented the difficulties of the sick (35:13-14). Habakkuk wrestled with the Lord because of the violence and injustice he witnessed around him (Habakkuk 1:2-4). Nehemiah, living in exile, "wept and mourned for days" when he heard that his homeland was in ruins (Nehemiah 1:4-11). As prophets like Isaiah, Jeremiah, and Micah preached hard truths, they did so with tears and tender hearts, lamenting the destruction they warned against (Isaiah 22:4; Jeremiah 9:1; Micah 1:8). Paul experienced "unceasing anguish" because of his unsaved relatives (Romans 9:1-5). And Jesus grieved the imminent desolation that Jerusalem would face (Luke 13:34-35; 19:41-44). The Bible repeatedly portrays believers lamenting the anguish of others. They took the trouble they saw and turned it over to the Lord in honest prayer.

For over a year after Eli's death, our friend Fay sent us a card in the mail every couple of weeks. Her words were always few—she simply wanted us to know we were in her prayers. The growing stack of her cards became hard to contain and her handwriting became endearingly familiar. From a distance, she remained present. In the darkness, we weren't alone. She carried our sorrows by crying out to the Lord on our behalf.

You, too, can turn to prayer as an instinct of compassion. And lament can shape your words before the Lord. Weeping and wrestling with God should be a natural response to the suffering you see. So when you hear about others' trials—pause. Consider how to have an honest conversation with the Lord. Remember, we're typically inclined towards petition and praise. But don't skip past the pain and protest. Explain the difficulties you see and faithfully complain. Cry out to the Lord when you hear about oppression or war, poverty or injustice, violence or abuse, depression or anxiety, unbelief or rebellion, sickness or death. Others' grief ought to compel our groans. Learn to meet tragedy with a ministry of tears.[49]

Something that helps me weep with others is writing out a lament on their behalf. It has been as simple as writing their name along with a short protest like, "Why, Lord?" I leave it on my desk, or in a note in my phone, to keep them on my heart. I've also found Psalm 13 to be a helpful framework to write out a full lament. Its succinct and powerful language can easily be changed to fit the circumstances someone is going through. Here's an example, with names removed:

How long, O Lord, will you allow cancer to take those we love?

How long must we wait for you to make all things new?

Consider my friend and his family. Listen to their cries.

With death so close, comfort can feel so far away.

Help them, through their tears, to trust in your steadfast love.

Bring them to one day rejoice again in your salvation.

I will sometimes write out these laments just to help me pray and remember their situation. Other times I'll share it with the person to let them know I'm crying out with them. Either way, putting your prayer to paper may help you to lament thoughtfully for others.

Yet it can be hard to know what to say when you pray for others, especially when they suffer something you're unfamiliar with. There are several great resources that can provide words for your laments. The second volume of *Every Moment Holy* contains liturgies for a broad variety of trials and losses—from medical procedures, to national disasters, to suicide, to difficulties during the holidays. *Liturgies of Hope* is a book of prayers for, in the words of its subtitle, "the highs, the lows, and everything in between." Those lows include experiences like financial burdens, worry over physical health, grief, and waking up in the middle of the night. *Sheltering Mercy* and *Endless Grace* are books of prayers, inspired by the Psalms, that maintain the honest wrestling with God in the midst of various struggles. And we've already discussed the importance of saturating your prayers in the Psalms. You don't need to be original in your outcries for others—lean on the shared wisdom and creativity of other believers to lament the suffering you see.

As you walk with sufferers, make their sorrows your own by crying out to the Lord for them. Your "thoughts and prayers" need not be vague or reserved—they can be honest, specific, and bold.

LISTEN

Even as we lament for others, we're still confronted with this daunting reality: *what do I say?* Our hearts break and we grasp for words that might offer relief. It's important to weigh what we say carefully, but there's a deeper question to consider. Our first response should not be a desperate search for the right thing to say—we ought to consider how we can help *them* speak. Lament has shown us that for pain to find comfort, it needs a voice. Sufferers need someone who will listen.

The Lord shows us how compassion begins with hearing. When the enslaved Israelites lamented, "God heard their groaning" (Exodus 2:24). While Job's friends rushed in with hasty words, the Lord listened patiently as his servant grieved, waiting until chapter 38 to respond. The psalms are full of lamenting believers who begged God to listen and praised him for hearing their cry—like when David prayed in Psalm 28: "Hear the voice of my pleas for mercy ... Blessed be the LORD! For he has heard the voice of my pleas for mercy" (v 2, 6). And Jesus' ministry put God's compassionate hearing on full display. When sufferers cried out to Jesus for mercy, healing, and deliverance, they always found an empathetic ear. How does God respond to cries of pain? He listens.

Hurting people need to be heard. And you can be an extension of God's mercy by offering them your ear. Be someone who will listen and help them lament.

After we lost Eli, I knew it would be good to meet with a counselor. But my first experience caused more harm than healing. The counselor did most of the talking and made insensitive remarks. Despite the frustration, I couldn't let him dictate my view on counseling. So I moved on to someone different. Apprehension loomed over me as I anticipated our initial appointment. Was this going to be another waste of time and money? Would this counselor listen?

The tension was tangible as I stepped into his office. But his first words erased my anxiety. "Tell me about Eli." His simple invitation struck with profound empathy. He wanted to hear about my story, my sorrow, and my son. Through tears I shared about the pride and pain wrapped around my soul. And this became the first of many sessions where my heartache was gently heard.

My counselor had decades of experience and a clinical focus on anxiety, depression, and complicated grief. His expertise helped me navigate the wild terrain of bereavement. But he wasn't my only listener. Several people close to us braved the darkness and listened as Jillian and I groaned. None of our friends or family were experts in grief. Yet they sat with us patiently and helped us voice our pain.

Listening is a rare gift, but it's something we all can cultivate. It's the core of great counseling, the heart of good friendship, and a sign of selfless love. When you offer your ear to someone in pain, you reflect our compassionate God. When someone you know is suffering, extend this simple invitation. *Tell me about it.*

So where does lament come in? It can be your guide as you help others voice their pain. Lament's four aspects can provide a framework for empathetic listening.

Allow sufferers to *explain their pain*. Assume that you don't understand what they're going through. Rather, ask them what they're feeling and why. You can show them the vivid imagery of biblical lament and see if it resonates with their difficulties. Encourage them to articulate their own sorrows like people do in the Bible. Give them the opportunity to put words to their experience.

Invite them to *express their protests*. Let them know it's okay to struggle with the Lord and that there's a faithful way to complain. What is it about their suffering that doesn't sit well with them? What confuses them about the Lord? What about God and his promises do they wrestle with? Point them to the protests of people like David, Habakkuk, and Jesus to free them up to do the same. Resist the need to resolve the tension. Instead, linger in the struggle with them in love.

Ask about their *earnest petitions*. Remind them that it's appropriate to ask the Lord to change their circumstances. What are they hoping for? How do they want God to act? Like Jesus in the Garden of Gethsemane, help them see that contentment doesn't come through silencing our desires. We may not receive the answer we want. But we can wrestle with the Lord and fight to trust him as we voice our requests.

Walk with them patiently towards *eventual praise*. Is there anything about the Lord that gives them comfort or hope right now? Even things that don't feel true can provide an anchor in the storm. But they might also need to hear that praise does not need to be forced or immediate—it can come in time through the process of lament. This is why the greatest thing you can do as a friend is help them wrestle honestly with the Lord. So ask them what it could look like for them to bring their laments to God. And wait with them as they struggle from pain to praise.

These types of questions will not typically be answered in one conversation. Nor are these the only things to be asking and listening for. But this can lead you in the right direction as you endeavor to be "quick to hear [and] slow to speak" (James 1:19). Offer the comfort of the Lord by asking, listening, and helping them lament.

ACT

Lamenting and listening are powerful gestures of love. Sometimes, hearing others and hurting with them is all we can do. But lament can also compel us towards further acts of compassion.

Some of the biblical examples mentioned earlier put this on display. Nehemiah's lamenting led him to rebuild the ruins of Jerusalem. Paul's sorrow for the unsaved provoked his relentless evangelism. And the groans of Christ resulted in the ultimate act of love, his death on the cross. When we internalize and vocalize others' sorrow, our feet can't stay still. Lament moves us to act.

To be clear, our efforts shouldn't aim to fix what's broken in our friends. While some situations can improve with practical support, many circumstances can't be solved by our strength. Struggles like depression, cancer, anxiety, trauma, and grief often lay far beyond our capacity. But we can still offer profound comfort and help.

And listening through the lens of lament deepens our ability to provide thoughtful support. If you take the time to become familiar with their particular difficulties and desires, you can love sufferers in ways that meet their practical, emotional, and spiritual needs. We should still proceed with humility and hold our efforts with an open hand—everyone suffers differently and each situation is unique. But lamenting with them can help you learn how best to care for them. So lean in to the opportunity to extend compassion when calamity strikes.

One of the first gifts we received for Eli was from our friend, Sarah, and was inspired by lament. Our situation devastated her. As she cried out to the Lord for us, she couldn't shake an image from her mind—Scripture's portrayal of Jesus as both Lion and Lamb. She pleaded with God to display both his lion-like power on our behalf and his lamb-like gentleness. And her cries moved her towards creative compassion. Sarah made Eli a quilt that proclaimed he was known and loved. Its warm colors contrasted the darkness we faced. A chevron design and arrows in the pattern paid tribute to Eli's nickname, "our little warrior." She embroidered in Hebrew, "Eleazar," the name that inspired us to call him Eli. And she included the images that pervaded her prayers—a lion and a lamb. Sarah had no idea that I had wanted lion and lamb prints for Eli's nursery, an ache that made her quilt a perfect gift.

Not only did the quilt express Sarah's love and loyalty, it also created for our family a liturgy of joyful sorrow. When Jillian was pregnant with Eli, she would cover up with it and lay it on her stomach when lying down. She wanted to wrap our son in the love he deserved. Lament became tangible compassion.

Many others came alongside us in various, creative ways. Several friends expressed their love through handmade keepsakes. Others drew, painted, or paid artists to make something for Eli. Some wrote poetry, sent cards, or bought gifts that honored our son and parenthood. Our best friend, a professional photographer, rushed to the hospital to document the only time our family would hold Eli. Several people displayed those pictures in their home or office to remember him daily. One friend dedicated his first published children's book to Eli, a story about finding beauty in the midst of struggle.[50] Other friends put a note with Eli's name in the Wailing Wall during their visit to Israel. Several people bought Jillian jewelry to honor her motherhood and our son. Another friend still sends flowers every year on Eli's birthday and Mother's Day. And Eli will forever occupy a place in our extended family. His grandparents, uncles, aunts, and cousins remember him with affection and speak his name with pride.

And then there was the heartfelt provision of practical help. People bought us groceries, gave gift cards, and dropped off meals. Friends cleaned our house while we were in the hospital to ease the burden when we got home.

Family and friends gave financially in order to take care of Eli's funeral and burial costs. Others made donations in Eli's name to organizations that come alongside grieving parents. And we were able to take a trip for rest and reprieve because of the generosity of those around us.

The help we received as grieving parents will not translate to every situation. I'm also aware that we experienced an outpouring of love that can be rare to come across. But I share these examples to compel more people to be thoughtful and creative with their care. The love of Christ marks communities with compassion that comes near and stays close.

So how can you enter into someone else's suffering? Here are two areas to consider as you let lament guide you forward.

Serve. Consider how their suffering makes life difficult right now. Are there any burdens you can lift? How can you serve them practically? Even if it's not directly related to their struggle, offering help can provide some relief and remind them they're not alone. Are there ways you can simply bless them in the midst of their pain? What do they typically enjoy or appreciate? Your generosity can bring some respite when rest and joy can be hard to find.

Remember. Find ways to keep them on your mind. Set reminders to pray for them and let them know. Think about their day-to-day—what upcoming events or occasions might be harder because of what they're going through? Will holidays or anniversaries be difficult? Mark your calendar and tell them you're thinking of them. Send them cards or gifts to remind them they're not forgotten. Think of creative ways to express your love and acknowledge their difficulties. Even from a distance, you can come close.

Those who walked with us admit that they were nervous about saying or doing the wrong thing. After all, it's risky and uncomfortable to weep with those who weep. It would have been easy to pull back in silence or offer shallow consolations. But they braved the brokenness with us. Love feels the weight of others' pain. It considers the details of their sorrow. And it wades through the discomfort to offer presence in the darkness. Compassion calls for your courage—and sometimes creativity—to honor others' heartache. And don't forget that one of the most powerful things you can do is keep crying out to the Lord and showing up to listen. Groan on behalf of others and take on their sorrows as your own. And let your mourning motivate action.

Coming alongside someone who's hurting can feel intimidating or complicated—but my nephew showed me how simple it can be. Jansen was only eight when Eli died. When his parents talked about the funeral, it wasn't even a question for him. He interrupted them to say he was going. When they reminded him about his friend's party happening at the same time, he insisted. "No. I'm going to Eli's service. My friend will have other birthday parties."

We faced the deepest agony of our lives, but Jansen's fierce loyalty flickered a light in the darkness. At such a young age, he bravely stepped into death's shadow. His presence proclaimed his commitment to us and the cousin he never got to meet. But he didn't just attend the funeral. He also felt the weight of our sorrow.

As the funeral ended, Jillian and I sat in front of Eli's casket, immobilized by grief. Friends and family lined up to give us hugs and offer their heartfelt sympathy. To be honest, I don't remember much of that moment. But I will never forget my encounter with Jansen. As he approached to give us a hug, Jansen wept. He didn't say anything as we embraced—he didn't have to. The tears streaming down his face said more than words ever could. His open display of grief declared his love for us and Eli. Jansen's presence and tears powerfully reflected the heart of Jesus and whispered hope in our sorrow.

This is the simple power of Christlike compassion. Show up. Shed tears. Lament, listen, and love.

HURTING WITH HOPE

His question stung with blunt curiosity: "Are you the ones who lost a child?"

The person asking was attempting to place us—trying to determine if he knew who we were. Only weeks had passed since Eli's death, but that was enough time for us to obtain this new title. Yes, we were "the ones who had lost a child." We could now be identified by who we no longer had.

At first, this label confused my sense of identity. I became a father when Jillian became pregnant. But who was I now that our only child was gone? To claim "I *am* a dad" felt both true and inaccurate at the same time; to say "I *was* a dad" seemed just as imprecise and incomplete. Death disoriented me and made its permanent mark on my parenthood.

Suffering can sometimes feel like it defines you. Your identity gets branded by whatever scrapes your soul—anxiety, depression, abuse, illness, death. So not only do your struggles alter how you live, they can also make you wrestle with who you are.

Some of Jesus' closest friends faced a similar identity crisis. Recall the scene at Lazarus' funeral in John 11. After his death, Martha was described as "the sister of the dead man" (John 11:39). The grave forced new labels on this grieving family—cold titles that shuddered with harsh reality.

But death's power could not change their identity in Christ—they were fiercely loved by Jesus.

You see this woven all throughout their story. When Mary and Martha asked Jesus for help, they identified their dying brother by his most important quality: Lazarus was "he whom you love" (v 3). Jesus' affection extended to Lazarus' sisters as well: "Now Jesus loved Martha and her sister and Lazarus" (v 5). Jesus' loving resolve to attend the funeral was a costly decision, as it put him in the vicinity of those who were trying to kill him (v 8). At Lazarus' tomb, onlookers saw Jesus' compassion through his tears, exclaiming, "See how he loved him!" (v 36). And his miracle of raising Lazarus from the grave paved the way for Jesus' ultimate act of love—it was such a powerful sign that his enemies now determined to put him to death (v 45-53). By bringing Lazarus out of the tomb, Jesus was triggering his own crucifixion. This family, wounded by loss, was marked by something deeper—Jesus' sacrificial love.

Though I struggled with the label at first, I no longer shy away from being "the one who lost a child." I hate that death took away my son. But it's an honor to be marked as Eli's father. And I know that "bereaved dad" is not my only identity. Because of Christ, I'm also a beloved son. My Savior has owned my sorrow as his own—and resurrection hope bears the weight of my grief.

Various trials may mark your identity. But Jesus' love shifts who you are, binding you to hope. Bearing the label of Christ's beloved helps you navigate the darkness with these final three reminders.

Your pain is real. Lazarus' family was deeply aware of Jesus' love for them. But this did not diminish their heartache. And Jesus did not discount their despair—he joined them in their grief (v 33-35). Likewise, your identity in Christ does not lessen the sorrows of life. As we have seen all throughout this book, burdened believers engage and express their difficulties. So don't give in to the pressure to dismiss your suffering. Strong faith weeps. And Jesus' love promises that your griefs matter to God. He is always poised with patience as you seek to explain your pain.

Your wrestling is welcome. Mary and Martha knew that Jesus' love was not meant to dissolve the tension they felt with him. No, it ensured a secure relationship where they could bring him their faithful complaints. They both had the same cry before Jesus: "If you had been here, my brother would not have died" (v 21, 32). Their heartache echoes the laments found all throughout Scripture. God is not put off by your honesty. He permits your protests and petitions. So resist the temptation to turn away from the Lord. Instead, tell God your troubles, bring him all your perplexities, and cry out your desperate requests. Wrestle with God—but do so with the assurance that your groans are covered in grace.

Your hope is sure. By calling Lazarus from the tomb, Jesus sealed his own death. Yet this exchange also led to one last identity change for Lazarus. He who was once "the dead man" (v 39) became known as the one "whom Jesus had raised from the dead" (12:1). If you're in Christ, you belong to the one who has power over the grave. Your laments ring out under the banner of a resurrected King. When he returns, all eventual praise will turn eternal. Joy will no longer be eclipsed by sorrow. And death will finally die. You can trust the Lord through tears, knowing that Jesus will one day wipe them away. So struggle faithfully. Groan boldly. Hurt with hope.

LAMENTS IN
THE PSALMS

Below is a list of all the laments in the Psalms, curated from various scholarly sources. As you read through these laments you will notice a broad range of emotion and experience. You'll see struggles with loneliness (142:4); depression (88); abuse (22); abandonment (13); weakness (109:24); violence (59); injustice (10); sleeplessness (77:1-4); sin (51); corruption (14:3); war (79:3-4); poverty (12:5); sickness (6:2); grief (31:9); fear (55:5); disrespect (123:4); chronic suffering (88:15); waiting (6:3); interpersonal conflict (120:2); hatred from others (109); and difficulties with God (13:1), family (27:10), friends (38:11), and enemies (42:9). Of course, most laments contain overlapping struggles that can't be neatly categorized, as it is with life. But I trust that their wrestling will enable your own.

LAMENTS IN THE PSALMS

3	17	41	58	77	94	140
4	22	42–43	59	79	102	141
5	25	44	60	80	108	142
6	26	51	61	83	109	143
7	28	53	64	85	120	
9–10	31	54	69	86	123	
12	35	55	70	88	126	
13	38	56	71	89	130	
14	39	57	74	90	137	

Total: 60

Curated from:

W.H. Bellinger, *Psalms: Reading and Studying the Book of Praises* (Hendrickson, 1990), p 23.

Glenn Pemberton, *Hurting with God: Learning to Lament with the Psalms* (Abilene Christian University Press, 2012), p 241-246.

Mark Vroegop, *Dark Clouds, Deep Mercy: Discovering the Grace of Lament* (Crossway, 2019), Appendix 2.

LAMENT SONGS

It's difficult to find lament songs, especially for use in corporate worship. But several people have written biblically-informed songs filled with honest wrestling and hope. I put together this playlist as a place to start for individuals and congregations to worship through lament. While churches might need to become familiar with the concept of lament, most of these songs should be teachable for congregational singing. And if you listen to this list personally, know that it's order is intentional—the laments toward the beginning tend to be more sorrowful, while the songs at the end turn more toward rejoicing and hope.

- "Lament" by Seacoast Worship

- "Wake Up, Jesus" by The Porter's Gate

- "Arise, Lord" by Clint Watkins

- "Reason to Sing" by All Sons & Daughters

- "Rise Up" by Bifrost Arts

- "Lord from Sorrows Deep I Call (Psalm 42)" by Matt Boswell and Matt Papa

- "How Long, O Lord" by City Hymns

- "How Long, O Lord, How Long (Psalm 13)" by Sovereign Grace Music

- "Though You Slay Me" by Shane & Shane

- "Abide with Me" by The Worship Initiative

- "Drive Out the Darkness" by The Porter's Gate

- "From the Depths of Woe (Psalm 130)" by Indelible Grace Music

- "Weep with Me" by Rend Collective

- "Dear Refuge of My Weary Soul" by Sovereign Grace Music

- "Purge Me" by Urban Doxology

- "Let Me Find Thee" by Indelible Grace Music

- "How Long?" by Bifrost Arts

- "O God of Mercy, Hear Our Plea" by Sovereign Grace Music

- "Psalm 126" by Sojourn Music

- "Psalm 42 (Loudest Praise)" by Shane & Shane
- "Come, Lord Jesus, Come" by The Worship Initiative

I've curated these songs and more into two spotify playlists, which can be accessed using the following QR codes.

Personal Wrestling:

Corporate Laments:

ENDNOTES

1 J. Alasdair Groves & Winston T. Smith, *Untangling Emotions* (Crossway, 2019), p 24, emphasis added.

2 Philip Yancey, *Prayer* (Zondervan, 2006), p 66.

3 J.I. Packer & Carolyn Nystrom, *Praying* (InterVarsity Press, 2006), p 181.

4 Tim Keller, "Truth, Tears, Anger, and Grace." (Sermon, Redeemer Presbyterian Church, 09/16/2021).

5 Nicholas Wolterstorff, *Lament for a Son* (Grand Rapids, 1987), p 5-6.

6 Dane Ortlund, *Gentle and Lowly* (Crossway, 2020), p 46

7 Rebekah Eklund, *Jesus Wept: The significance of Jesus' Laments in the New Testament* (T&T Clark, 2016), p 31.

8 Paul imitates Jesus' Gethsemane prayer in 2 Corinthians 12:7-10.

9 Glenn Pemberton, *Hurting with God: Learning to Lament with the Psalms* (Abilene Christian University Press, 2012), p 51.

10 Pemberton, *Hurting with God*, p 48.

11 Wolterstorff, *Lament for a Son*, p 80.

12 I am indebted to Tim Mackie for pointing this out to me in his sermon, "Praying Through Our Pain" (Door of Hope Church, 05/26/2013).

13 Groves and Smith, *Untangling Emotions*, p 102-103.

14 Pemberton, *Hurting with God*, p 151.

15 Scott Harrower & Sean M. McDonough, *A Time for Sorrow* (Hendrickson Academic, 2019), p 16.

16 Robert Smith, "Belting out the Blues as Believers: The Importance of Singing Lament," *Themelios*, April 2017, p 97.

17 For example: Psalm 88 lacks praise, Psalm 77 lacks petition, and Psalm 13 enfolds the pain in its protest and petition. Psalm 44 begins with praise, moves to protest, then ends in petition; Psalm 10 puts protest before explained pain. Rarely does a lament psalm follow a strict order.

18 For example, see Psalm 55:2; Psalm 64:1; Psalm 142:2; Job 7:11; Job 10:1; Habakkuk 2:1; Jeremiah 12:1.

19 Harold L. Senkbeil, *Christ and Calamity* (Lexham Press, 2020), p 25.

20 See Psalms 78, 95, and 106, as well as Hebrews 3:7 – 4:7 and 1 Corinthians 10:6-13.

21 Eric Ortlund, *Suffering Wisely and Well* (Crossway, 2022), p 23.

22 Christopher Ash, *Trusting God in the Darkness* (Crossway, 2021), p 19.

23 Ash, *Trusting God in the Darkness*, p 131.

24 Derek Kidner, *Psalms 73 – 150* (InterVarsity Press Academic, 2014), p 313.

25 "At the Cross" by Isaac Watts.

26 You see a similar reality in his letter to the Philippians, a book overflowing with joy. He tells his readers: "Rejoice in the Lord always; again I will say, rejoice" (Philippians 4:4). Yet he also shares about the "sorrow upon sorrow" (2:27) he would have experienced if his friend had died.

27 Groves and Smith, *Untangling Emotions*, p 45, emphasis added.

28 O. Palmer Robertson, *The Prophets of Nahum,*

Habakkuk, and Zephaniah (Eerdmans, 1990), p 141.

29 Gerald H. Wilson, *Psalms Volume 1, The NIV Application Commentary* (Zondervan, 2002), p 23.

30 To be clear, the book of Psalms is more than a hymnbook—these prayers and songs tell the story of God's people and their hope in a suffering King, ultimately pointing to the person and work of Jesus (Luke 24:44).

31 Christopher Ash, *Teaching Psalms: Volume 1 – From text to Message* (Proclamation Trust Media, 2017), p 21.

32 Bob Kauflin, *Worship Matters: Leading Others to Encounter the Greatness of God* (Crossway, 2008), p 66.

33 The ESV Study Bible (Crossway Bibles, 2008), p 935.

34 Mark Vroegop, *Dark Clouds, Deep Mercy: Discovering the Grace of Lament* (Crossway, 2019), p 160.

35 Pemberton, *Hurting with God*, p 39.

36 Denise Hopkins, *Journey through the Psalms* (Chalice Press, 2002), p 204.

37 Hopkins, *Journey through the Psalms*, p 157.

38 For example, many songs based on Psalm 42 omit the question the writer has for God. "Why have you forgotten me?" (Psalm 42:9).

39 Hopkins, *Journey Through the Psalms*, p 204.

40 Tim Keller, *Walking with God through Pain and Suffering* (Riverhead, 2013), p 246.

41 Matt Merker, *Corporate Worship: How the Church Gathers as God's People* (Crossway, 2021), p 62-63.

42 Walter Brueggemann, *Spirituality of the Psalms* (Augsburg Fortress, 2002), p 23.

43 Carl Trueman, "What Can Miserable Christians Sing?" *Themelios*, February 2000, 160.

44 See Mark 5:35-43 and 9:2-8.

45 C.S. Lewis, *A Grief Observed* (HarperCollins, 1994), p 52-53.

46 Wolterstorff, *Lament for a Son*, p 51.

47 For example, see Psalm 3, 13, or 22.

48 For example, see Psalm 28 and compare verses 1-5 with verses 6-9.

49 Though I don't know if he coined this term, I first heard it during Tim Keller's sermon, "Truth, Tears, Anger, and Grace" (Redeemer Presbyterian Church, 9/16/2001).

50 J.P. Hostetler, *The Sky Belongs to the Dreamers* (Atmosphere Press, 2019).

thegoodbook
COMPANY

BIBLICAL | RELEVANT | ACCESSIBLE

At The Good Book Company, we are dedicated to helping Christians and local churches grow. We believe that God's growth process always starts with hearing clearly what he has said to us through his timeless word—the Bible.

Ever since we opened our doors in 1991, we have been striving to produce Bible-based resources that bring glory to God. We have grown to become an international provider of user-friendly resources to the Christian community, with believers of all backgrounds and denominations using our books, Bible studies, devotionals, evangelistic resources, and DVD-based courses.

We want to equip ordinary Christians to live for Christ day by day, and churches to grow in their knowledge of God, their love for one another, and the effectiveness of their outreach.

Call us for a discussion of your needs or visit one of our local websites for more information on the resources and services we provide.

Your friends at The Good Book Company

thegoodbook.com | thegoodbook.co.uk
thegoodbook.com.au | thegoodbook.co.nz
thegoodbook.co.in